Calendar

Chinese Characters	Code		Corresponding Dates in Solar Calendar						
			1998 Tiger	1999 Rabbit	2000 Dragon	2001 Snake	2002 Horse	2003 Sheep	2004 Monkey
灶君節	F	h	22/1	9/2	30/1	18/1	5/2	26/1	15/1
農曆新年	F	h	28/1	16/2	5/2	24/1	12/2	1/2	22/1
車公誕	GB	p	30/1	18/2	7/2	26/1	14/2	3/2	24/1 leap
元宵			11/2	2/3	19/2	7/2	26/2	15/2	5/2 2nd Moon
土地誕	O	ph	28/2	19/3	7/3	24/2	15/3	4/3	21/2 (22/3)
洪聖誕	GB	p	11/3	30/3	18/3	7/3	26/3	15/3	3/3 (2/4)
觀音誕	GB	p	17/3	5/4	24/3	13/3	1/4	21/3	9/3 (8/4)
清明節	FA	o	5/4	5/4	4/4	5/4	5/4	5/4	4/4
北帝誕	GB	p	30/3	18/4	7/4	27/3 leap	15/4	4/4	21/4
天后誕	GB	p	19/4	8/5	27/4	16/4 4th Moon	5/5	24/4	11/5
長洲飽山節	HG	p	Dates chosen by Divination						
浴佛節	B	i	3/5 leap	22/5	11/5	30/4 (30/5)	19/5	8/5	26/5
譚公誕	GB	p	3/5 5th Moon	22/5	11/5	30/4 (30/5)	19/5	8/5	26/5
端午節	O	p	30/5 (28/6)	18/6	6/6	25/6	15/6	4/6	22/6
關帝誕	GB	p	7/6 (6/7)	26/6	14/6	3/7	23/6	12/6	30/6
侯王誕	GB	p	28/7	18/7	7/7	26/7	15/7	5/7	22/7
魯班誕	GB	i	4/8	25/7	14/7	2/8	22/7	12/7	29/7
觀音誕	GB	p	10/8	31/7	20/7	8/8	28/7	18/7	4/8
七姐節	O	h	28/8	17/8	6/8	25/8	15/8	4/8	22/8
盂蘭節	HG	p	5/9	25/8	14/8	2/9	23/8	12/8	30/8
中秋節	F	h	5/10	24/9	12/9	1/10	21/9	11/9	28/9
齊天大聖誕	O		6/10	25/9	13/9	2/10	22/9	12/9	29/9
孔聖誕	O	i	17/10	6/10	24/9	13/10	3/10	23/9	10/10
重陽節	FA		28/10	17/10	6/10	25/10	14/10	4/10	22/10
觀音誕	GB	p	7/11	27/10	16/10	4/11	24/10	14/10	1/11
冬至	F	h	22/12	22/12	21/12	22/12	22/12	22/12	21/12
太平清醮	HG	p	Dates chosen by Divination						

o *Others*
p *Public*
h *Home*
i *Institution*

CHINESE FESTIVALS

IN HONG KONG

CHINESE FESTIVALS

IN HONG KONG

Barbara E. Ward & Joan Law

Published by The Guidebook Company Limited

Text by Barbara E. Ward
Designed by Joan Law

ISBN 962-217-304-7

Produced by Twin Age Limited
Printed in China

Acknowledgements
The authors would like to thank the South China Morning Post Limited for their generous support without which this second edition of Chinese Festivals in Hong Kong would not have been possible. Thanks are due to Ch'oi Chi-ch'eung for his valuable suggestions and comments for the updating of this edition. Thanks again to all the people who helped make this book possible. They include Magnus Bartlett, Edmond Ch'an Hau-leung, Ch'an Wing-hoi, Chang Tsong-zung, David Faure, Ng Yuk-ch'ing, Kate Sandweiss, Evelyn Sebastian, So Yui-hung, David Yung, and the Taoists priests, village elders, committee members, villagers, and participants in festivals all over Hong Kong whose unfailing kindness and hospitality they can never repay.

In memory of Barbara E. Ward

Festival Map

Moon One

New Year's Day
most temples

Birthday of God of Wealth
Wong Tai Sin Temple, Lam Tsuen Valley

Birthday of Ch'e Kung
Ch'e Kung Temple, Shatin

Yuen Siu (Lantern Festival)
Ancestral Halls, clan, neighbourhood, and district associations in the New Territories and outlying islands

Moon Two

Birthday of T'o Tei Kung
Almost anywhere, especially the villages of the New Territories and the older parts of the town

Birthday of Hung Shing Kung
Hung Shing Kung temples at:
Ap Lei Chau, Tai O (Lantau Island), Kau Sai Chau, Sha Lo Wan (Lantau Island)

Birthday of Koon Yam
Koon Yam temples at: Kwu Tung, Pak Sha Wan (Hebe Haven)

Moon Three

Birthday of Pak Tai
Pak Tai temples at:
Stanley, Tsing Yi Island, Cheung Chau, Mong Tseng Wai

Birthday of T'in Hau
T'in Hau temples at:
Sai Wan (Cheung Chau), Joss House Bay, Yuen Long, Ping Che, Leung Shuen Wan, Tsing Yi Island, Sai Kung, Sok Kwu Wan (Lamma Island)

Ch'ing Ming Festival
(usually 5 or 6 April, may be in Moon Two)
Cemeteries at:
Wo Hop Shek, Aberdeen, Chai Wan, Cheung Chau, Peng Chau and all over the New Territories

Moon Four

Birthday of the Lord Buddha
Buddhist monasteries at:
Castle Peak, Shatin, Lantau Island

Birthday of T'am Kung
T'am Kung Temple, Shau Kei Wan

Cheung Chau Bun Festival
Pak Tai Temple, Cheung Chau

Moon Five

Dragon Boat Festival
Boat races at:
Stanley, Shau Kei Wan, Aberdeen, Chai Wan, Tai Po, Sai Kung, Yau Ma Tei, Tung Chung, Tsim Sha Tsui East

Birthday of Kwan Tai
All Kwan Tai temples

Moon Six

Birthday of Hau Wong
Hau Wong temples at:
Kowloon City, Tai O (Lantau Island)

Birthday of Lu Pan
Lu Pan Temple, Kennedy Town

Enlightenment of Koon Yam
Koon Yam Temple, Pak Sha Wan (Hebe Haven), Shek O

Moon Seven

Seven Sisters' Festival
Anywhere. Temple on Peng Chau Island

Yue Laan (Hungry Ghosts Festival)
Most districts all over Hong Kong

Moon Eight

Mid-Autumn Festival
Victoria Park, Tai Hang, Stanley Beach, and most other public spaces

Monkey God Festival
Temple at Sau Mau Ping (Sau Mau Ping Road Playground)

Birthday of Hau Wong
Hau Wong Temple, Tung Chung (Lantau Island)

Birthday of Confucius
Confucius Hall Middle School, Caroline Hill Road, Causeway Bay

Moon Nine

Ch'ung Yeung Festival
The Peak, Wo Hop Shek Cemetery and cemeteries all over the New Territories

Remembrance of Koon Yam
Koon Yam temples at:
Kwu Tung, Pak Sha Wan (Hebe Haven)

Moon Eleven

Winter Solstice
(usually 21st or 22nd December)
Celebrations at home

Moon Twelve

Kitchen God Visits Heaven
Celebrations at home

New Year's Eve
Flower Markets at:
Victoria Park, Kai Tak Amusement Park, Shatin, Tai Po, Yuen Long

Contents

Names of the member-villagers at the festival are written on a long paper scroll which will be sent to heaven in flames on the back of a paper horse. Before it is sent, the Taoist priests have to chant every single name out loud so that the gods may know whom to bless. The villagers listen anxiously to make sure that their own family names are not missed out.

天

Putting body and soul together? Taai Si Wong's trunk is taken to join his head and legs. Preparing for the Hungry Ghosts Festival.

Preface

In the ten years since *Chinese Festivals in Hong Kong* was first published, Hong Kong has seen many changes. Although the rites of these traditional festivals remain basically the same, some of the elderly Taoist priests and craftsmen have retired, and some have passed away. This updated edition is intended to record the living heritage of the festivals as they are performed today.

The idea of this book started almost ten years ago when I was searching for a subject for my final design project at the Hong Kong Polytechnic. A friend of mine asked me to take pictures at a small village festival for him. This was the first time that I had ever gone to one of these festivals, and I hardly knew what to expect.

When I arrived, the huge colourful *flower boards* and the drums and gongs caught my attention. The villagers had put up three *matsheds* in an open area, one for the *gods*, one for the opera performances and one as a communal kitchen. Every single activity attracted me: old people chatting with each other, men and women helping in the organizing, and children running in and out of the *matsheds*. They were all enjoying themselves, and the friendly atmosphere made me feel that I could just be one of them. I grew up in the city, and had not realized that the villagers were so friendly.

Some men were dressed in red robes and were chanting along with the rhythm of the music. I was told these were the *Taoist* priests. They were the experts hired to perform the ceremonies.

While I was enjoying the music, three little boys came up to me and asked me to take their pictures. After I had done so, they called in a group of other children as well. The ten of them led me through the *matsheds* and we went backstage at the opera *matshed*. They said it was like New Year, with all the noise and colours. They told me the fearsome papier-mâché figure holding the writing brush at the entrance of the village was supposed to watch over the *ghosts* and to write down their names. At the end of the festival this figure would be burnt and sent back to Hell with all the *ghosts* in the area.

The ceremonies lasted four days. The villagers, after several days of abstinence from meat, started sharing roast pigs and chickens at the Big Feast. The entire festival came to an end, and every villager went home with a peaceful and happy heart.

All festivals are similar to this one that I attended. The main aim is to honour the *gods* or the *ancestors*. People offer worship and opera performances and in return they ask for guidance and good fortune. However, the rites of each festival are different.

I became so interested in these festivals that I decided to visit the different groups of people involved. The handicraft that went into the papier-mâché figures attracted me most, and I started to visit the craftsmen who made them. I once watched an elderly craftsman making *Taai Si Wong* (the fearsome figure I saw) on the island of Peng Chau. He was making five figures for the Hungry Ghosts Festival that was to come. To my surprise, he had only one assistant to help him do the painting. At sixty years of age, the two months spent preparing these five figures must have been a strenuous task. He treated each one as an independent work of art. The colours that he used and the expressions of the figures were really striking. I asked if he would teach me the craft. He refused. He wanted to pass it on to his son who was only seven years old. He said that people were not competent, and that was why he seldom hired help to work for him. I found it sad that he kept the art to himself. I had noticed this before: fathers wanting to keep the craft within the family, but the sons finding it less attractive than regular occupations in the city. The craft would then die out, as many others already have.

Again when I was watching another festival on a cold winter night, the *Taoist* priests had to perform the rites in an open area. It was so cold that the villagers all stayed inside the opera *matshed* to enjoy themselves, leaving the poor *Taoist* priests in the cold. The chief priest was about eighty years old and the rest of them were all over sixty. Afterwards they told me that the situation would be much better if only they had younger priests in the field. They said that nowadays young people would not take this as their profession because it was a difficult one to learn. They have to learn to play the music, chant different prayers, make paper figurines, and write good calligraphy. Although no one likes to learn the skill, everyone wants the *Taoist* priests to perform when there is a festival. I realized then the importance of capturing these fading customs before they disappeared, and I began going regularly with my camera to the villagers' festivals.

Joan Law Mee Nar

Collecting 'dirt' in the symbolic rubbish boat during the Lantern Festival and the Chiu Festival. Men in blue gowns represent the village and follow the Taoists in their offerings and worship.

Introduction

Most of Hong Kong's public festivals are uproarious affairs thronged with people, riotous with colour, noise, and smoke. Whole roast pigs play an important part in them, as do *Dancing Lions, Unicorns* and hardboiled eggs dyed red. There is fortune telling and gambling and prayer. There are usually opera performances and processions and, of course, people — more and more and more people. A wonderful time is obviously being had by all, but usually there is nobody at hand to explain what it is all about....

That's where this book comes in. It is a kind of festival-watcher's handbook, a guide through the traditional year, designed to make it possible to tell which festival is which, who are the main participants, and what are the key symbols and their meanings. We have tried to tell some of the stories behind each festival, and describe what the participants actually do, why they do it, and how the whole event is organized.

First, however, we want to say a few words about Hong Kong festivals in general.

Hong Kong as a Centre of Chinese Festival Traditions

At first sight it is rather difficult to think of contemporary, industrialized Hong Kong as a centre of Chinese traditionalism. But so in fact it is. Especially as regards festivals.

Naturally, people in Hong Kong like to have the best of both East and West. Nobody objects to having a vacation at Christmas and Easter as well as Chinese New Year and Ch'ing Ming, but the holidays that really matter are the traditional festivals outlined in this book.

There are such a lot of them too. Hardly a month passes without two or three major occasions that large numbers of people in different parts of the territory feel bound to celebrate; the minor ones are uncountable. Certainly there are more celebrations today than there used to be before the Second World War, and the money spent on them has been increasing every year, faster than the rate of inflation.

Nevertheless, it is natural to wonder how far the Chinese festivals one sees in contemporary Hong Kong resemble those that used to take place in traditional China.

The festivals described here certainly make use of modern techniques (electric light and microphones, for example); their organizers have to conform to certain modern regulations (to do with fire hazards, crowd control, and the like); and participants are likely to bring along video and tape-recorders, not to mention 35mm cameras with synchronized flash. In most other respects, however, things are very much as they always were. It is possible to read accounts of so-called 'temple fairs' in *Kwangtung Province* in the 1860s that apply in almost every particular to what can be seen in Hong Kong now.

Kwangtung Province is next door to Hong Kong, and most of Hong Kong's population comes from there. Left to themselves people everywhere tend to be very conservative in matters of religious custom, so it is not surprising that the festivals in Hong Kong today should still be similar to those of *Kwangtung* in the past. However, at present the differences are extreme. In China, virtually all spectacular festival activities have been forbidden for the last forty years; in Hong Kong they have not.

This fact in itself is the main reason why Hong Kong is, so unexpectedly, one of the very few places in the world where one can still see this kind of Chinese traditionalism. And, in spite of some recent signs of revival in China, it is likely to remain so. It is just not possible for a Marxist state to approve of the traditional beliefs in *gods* and spirits with which the majority of the more spectacular festivals are indissolubly linked. It is likely, therefore, that official sanction will only be given to the restoration of those festivals which are least connected with such beliefs.

The report that Dragon Boat races were held again in Nanning in 1982 supports this argument, for of all the public celebrations described in this book the Dragon Boat festival is the most 'secular'. The revival of *gods'* 'birthday' festivals, like the one described in Moon Two below, or full scale Hungry Ghosts Festivals, as in Moon Seven, would be quite another matter.

Who Takes Part?

It is important to recognise that the degree of participation in traditional festival activities varies a great deal in Hong Kong. Although some festivals are observed by almost everyone, there are others which are by no means so widely supported, and a great many Hong Kong people today know little or nothing about some of the more unusual traditional festivals and customs. These differences are partly connected with the fact that the Chinese population in Hong Kong is far from being homogeneous, and partly with the differing characteristics of the festivals themselves.

Chinese people in Hong Kong vary in their place of origin in China, and, of course, in other ways such as age, sex, income level, and standard of education. Festivals vary too. Some are common to the whole of China, others are local in origin and appeal; naturally the former have more followers than the latter. Some are based mainly on the home and family, like Christmas in most Western countries, and like Christmas relatively adaptable to modern, secular ways of thought. They include Chinese New Year, Ch'ing Ming, the Mid-Autumn (Moon) Festival, Ch'ung Yeung, and the Winter Solstice. The Dragon Boat Festival is also known to all, and, as it is a public holiday in Hong Kong, the races, which are officially sanctioned, are highly popular.

Some festivals are the concern of specialized religious institutions, such as *Buddhist* monasteries. These, naturally, cater to particular groups of avowed believers, inevitably limited in numbers. In any case, they are more or less private affairs, in complete contrast to the festivals of the popular religion which are organized in public places. These popular celebrations are the spectacular ones that catch the visitor's eye, the object of most festival-watching in Hong Kong. Though they are the particular concern of the local communities which organize them, they are truly public festivals, open to everyone, and the crowds which flock to them always include large numbers of people from all parts of the territory.

Most of these public festivals are centred on certain traditional temples, and the crowds therefore tend to be composed mainly of the more traditional elements of the population — the less well-off and less well-educated, the middle-aged and elderly, the women. But there are exceptions to every rule, and even though most educated people today affect to despise the public festivals and lack knowledge of the traditional customs associated with them, nevertheless there are many who do take part. Even today many young people go to accompany their mothers, and are not above sharing in the fortune-telling aspects of divination when they get there. Who is to know what these same young people will do later on when they in turn become parents?

Judging by the immense popularity of some of these festivals today, one hesitates to predict their early decline. Left to themselves, without governmental interference, they may well continue for many years to come.

Two final notes for would-be festival watchers:
First: keep your eyes open for the Religious Paper shops which sell incense, *spirit money*, candles and all the brilliantly coloured paper goods for temple offerings. Strictly ephemeral, since they are destined for burning, the paper goods are often still superb objects of folk art. And they are very cheap.
Second: festivals are expensive to run. There is always a collecting box, which makes it possible for any festival watcher to show thanks for the friendly hospitality that is generously given. Do not let yourself be put off by protests that 'it is not necessary' to put something in the box.

Note on spelling of Chinese words
The spelling of Chinese words in this book approximates the pronunciation of the local lingua franca which is Cantonese. Cantonese, widely spoken in *Kwangtung Province* and parts of Kwangsi, differs in many ways from the officially recognised form of Chinese, commonly known in English as Mandarin, which is based on the speech of Peking. Most writers in Western languages today use a form of 'romanization' that approximates to Mandarin pronunciation, but in a guidebook intended for practical use in Hong Kong Cantonese has obvious advantages.

Some aids to pronunciation
1. All consonants as in English except
   k', p', t', ch' (ts') as English k, p, t, ch (in church)
   k, p, t, ch (ts or tz) as English k (hard),
   b, d, j (in judge)
   s, sh both pronounced as English s
2. Most vowels more or less as in British English except
   i as 'ee' in seen
   ue as German 'ü'
   ui as the vowel in the second syllable of the French word 'fauteuil' (armchair)
3. Tones: Don't worry about them, unless you are trying to learn the language properly, in which case they are absolutely essential.

Taoist priest in his usual red ceremonial robe with Yin and Yang symbols on it. Once he has put on the ceremonial hat, 'T'ung T'in Ling Mo', he can communicate with the gods above.

Moon Twelve

The Month of Preparation

It is not always easy for a non-Chinese to understand the full moral, social, personal, and, indeed, cosmic significance of Chinese New Year.

Morally the keynote is renewal. The old year goes, and with it go old misfortunes and old wrongs; the new year comes and brings the chance for starting afresh. Socially it signifies reunion, the end of strife, the renewal of harmony. Personally and in business one hopes to pay off one's debts, tidy up all loose ends, and turn over a new leaf.

It is impossible to overestimate the importance of these ideas and the strength of the feeling that supports them. In traditional Chinese thinking they are tightly connected with such natural phenomena as the return of the *Yang* (already foreshadowed at the Winter Solstice) and the beginning of Spring. There is a cosmic process at work and human beings are part of it.

With such cosmic ideas as these (no matter how diluted they may have become for some people in the modern world), it is no wonder that the last month of the old year is given over to preparation. Besides, the New Year is a holiday, and there is much to get ready for that as well.

Domestic Preparations

The twentieth day of the Twelfth Moon is marked on the calendar as the 'day for sweeping the floors'. This means that a complete house cleaning begins in every home. Nothing is left untouched.

Like spring-cleaning in some Western countries, the operation is symbolic as well as practical. Removing the old year's dust and dirt stands also for getting rid of its shortcomings and disappointments. Material renovation signifies spiritual and social renewal.

Once the household cleaning is complete, Chinese housewives begin to stock up for the coming holiday period. Shops and markets are at their busiest, hawkers do a roaring trade, and all the streets are full of people. Having bought the ingredients the women must set to and cook them fast. Once the New Year dawns no one may use a knife, or indeed do any work at all for two days, so the days at the end of the month are the busiest of the year in the kitchen.

As all the shops will be closed for several days everyone is also busy buying gifts for friends and relatives, for the New Year in Hong Kong means presents — just like Christmas in the West — and the commercial impact is very much the same.

Day 24
Kitchen God
Visits Heaven

Day 30
New Year's Eve

Also:
Day 16
Mei Ah
(Last Sixteenth
Day of the Year)

Day 24 The Kitchen God Visits Heaven

The 24th (23rd in northern China) is the day on which the Kitchen God is supposed to leave for Heaven. The Kitchen (or Stove) God is a very old *god* indeed, a bit like another local guardian, T'o Tei Kung (see Moon Two) but more closely identified with the household than the house. He is also a kind of censor of the family's behaviour and once a year he is supposed to make a report to the *Jade Emperor* in Heaven.

So on this day when his picture is taken down for renewal it is ceremonially burned outside the kitchen to send him on his way. Before he goes he is worshipped with incense and candles, and given a delicious meal of sticky, sweet things — glutinous rice and honey or sugar and sometimes wine as well — smeared all over his mouth to make sure that what he says will be sweet and flattering.

It is a charming fancy, one which children love and half believe.

Paying Debts

Traditionally the Chinese have three dates in the year for paying debts: before New Year, the Dragon Boat Festival, and the Mid-Autumn Festival. The most important of these is Chinese New Year. Since many people live on credit, it is important to pay off all debts before the New Year dawns, so the last days of the month usually see a great scurrying around to collect and pay. That is why employees like to receive their annual gratuity of an extra month's pay well in advance.

Moral debts must also be paid. A good turn long forgotten may well call forth an unexpected return in these few days, and — more important by far — old quarrels are made up. If there is time, you should call on your friends before the end of the year, or at least send a New Year card.

Village women making New Year Cakes. The main ingredients are rice flour, brown sugar, and crushed roast peanuts. There are a number of wooden moulds with different propitious words on them usually referring to longevity, wealth, and the gift of sons.

Lucky Papers at the Door

On the last day of the month people put up their new luck-bringing papers. They include strips of red paper which are pasted on each side of the front door and across the lintel at the top. They always have propitious words written on them, usually referring to wealth, longevity, and the gift of sons. Over the lintel, more often than not, is the wish: May all your comings and goings be peaceful. On a junk: May you have a favourable wind all the way.

Lucky papers are not confined to doors. You can stick them anywhere in the house, and many people do. (Watch for diamond shapes in red and gold.) More important, perhaps, and certainly more striking, are the pictures that are posted at the same time — the new pair of Door Gods.

Brilliantly coloured when they are first put up, these two generals in full military array are demon slayers of the strongest kind. They are very old guardians, whose origins go back to an ancient *Taoist* legend about two brothers who lived under an enormous peach tree and protected mankind by catching demons and throwing them to tigers. It is said that the early magistrates in China used to put their carved peach wood images beside the *yamen* gates; later their pictures were painted there instead.

A different story links their origin with a famous emperor of the T'ang dynasty (618–907 AD) who suffered terrible nightmares about being attacked by demons. One night two of his generals begged to be allowed to spend the night in his room to drive the demons away. The plan succeeded and that night the emperor slept soundly. Later he commanded the court painter to make two portraits of the generals in full armour and hang them in his room instead. All his subjects ever afterwards have adopted the same method of keeping demons away.

The Flower Markets

Hong Kong is cold at this time of the year, and often wet, but flowers are everywhere. In the New Territories, flower farmers have been busy for at least two months coaxing their plants into blooming at exactly the right time. By the 26th day the Flower Markets open, and the roads are full of lorries piled high with little trees and plants.

The favourite plant to buy at New Year is a small peach tree just coming into bloom. Peach wood is the ancient and most potent enemy of demons and the peach itself is an emblem of longevity. As for the flowers, everyone likes to have flowers that are just opening to signify openness to all the good of the New Year. Next in popularity are bright green bushes laden with tiny oranges (kumquats), the Chinese characters for which sound the same as those for 'gold' and 'lucky'. Then there are waxen Hanging Bell Flowers, and fragrant white jonquils (called Water Fairies and often misnamed narcissus in English) which grow from bulbs placed in water without earth. Chrysanthemums, dahlias, and gladioli are also on sale.

The Flower Markets build up to a climax on New Year's Eve. If you stay late enough you can get good bargains, but for most people just pushing gently through the happy crowds, enjoying the anticipation of the coming holidays, buying a little here and there, is enough. No one should miss the Flower Markets on this night.

The best known ones are at Victoria Park on Hong Kong Island. There are smaller ones in the New Territories at Shatin, Tai Po and Yuen Long.

Top two — Walled villages in the New Territories: gateway with new 'lucky papers'. Bottom right — Hakka village woman offering incense at her newly decorated Ancestral Hall. Bottom left — Village women putting up the new Door Gods on New Year's Eve.

Operas for the ghosts, gods, and human beings to enjoy. Hoklo troupe in a scene from the Romance of the Three Kingdoms.

Moon One

Day 1
New Year's Day

Day 2
Birthday of
God of Wealth

Day 3
Birthday of
Ch'e Kung

Day 15
Yuen Siu:
Lantern Festival

Also:
Day 18
Star Gods
Festival

Day 1 New Year's Day

Where to go: Most temples are thronged with people around midnight on New Year's Eve. New Year itself is a family festival focused on the home; there are no public ceremonies.

Cosmic and Personal Renewal

This is the most important festival of all — the time of universal celebration and the principal occasion of family reunion. New Year is considered to be everybody's birthday, and everyone adds a year to his age on the seventh day (see *Yan Yat*, Glossary).

On the last night of the old year no one seems to go to bed. The streets are crammed with millions of happy people. There is no public marking of the moment of crossing from one year to the next, just a never-ending flow of good humoured crowds going nowhere in particular. Important things do happen, but they happen at home.

On New Year's Eve there is a special family dinner. This no one may miss — even those who have passed away are considered to be present in spirit, each one's place laid with a bowl and chopsticks before an empty chair. The details of what happens after dinner vary a little from family to family. Parents give their children little *red packets* with *'lucky money'* inside. Usually they are tucked under the pillow overnight. Children, in turn, make formal greetings to their parents.

In traditional homes in the old days, the head of the family would offer incense and pay respects to Heaven and Earth, the family *ancestors* and the guardian spirits in the evening, then lock and seal the doors of the house before midnight. This was done in order to keep out the evil spirits which were believed to be abroad at the passing of the year *(Kwoh Nin)*. This was also the occasion, and the reason, for letting off firecrackers in their hundreds of thousands. The doors were reopened at dawn and the master of the house then again worshipped Heaven, Earth, and the *ancestors*, as well as the Kitchen God who had just returned from his holiday in Heaven (see Moon Twelve).

Strictly speaking, New Year's Day itself is not a feast but a fasting day on which no meat should be eaten and even vegetables ought to be cooked in oil not lard. Fasting of this kind is a symbol of self-purification and renewal at the beginning of the year, like the bath that has to be taken on New Year's Eve and the new clothes that are always worn.

There are a number of other prohibitions at this time, all of them carrying the same ideas of symbolic renewal and starting afresh. For two days, no work (particularly no housework, especially sweeping) should be done. One must not even wash. No knives or scissors should be used, so all food has to be prepared beforehand. The symbolism of not cutting or not removing the brand new fortune of the brand new year is obvious. One must also be careful not to break or tear anything, and a fall or stumble is a shockingly bad omen.

Children are warned to watch their language since uttering 'bad' words is likely to presage disaster. This taboo applies not only to swearing but more particularly to mentioning the words for death, or sickness, or any other unlucky thing. Even other words that sound like 'bad' ones should not be allowed to pass one's lips. As Chinese is a language in which making puns is almost unavoidable, this prohibition poses very real problems. In some cases propitious sounding alternatives have been universally adopted; for example, the word for 'tongue' in Cantonese sounds exactly the same as the word for 'loss', so it has been replaced with another word which actually means 'profit'.

One of the most interesting customs of this same kind centres on the choice of *special foods* for the New Year period. Nearly every dish has a name which is a sign of good fortune.

Socially the main business of the New Year period is to visit and be visited by all one's relatives and friends. It is also the chance for young people to collect *red packets* of *'lucky money'*. Any married person on first being greeted after the New Year by an unmarried relative or friend is expected to hand over a *red packet*. Like American youngsters at Halloween, the children of Hong Kong have a rhyme that leaves no doubt about their hopeful expectations:

May the New Year be happy and wealthy for you
And bring us a big load of *red packets* too!

Days 2 and 3 The God of Wealth and the Birthday of Ch'e Kung

Where to go: The God of Wealth resides in the home, but he is also present in many temples and people can be seen visiting him there as well. The Ch'e Kung temple is at Shatin.

Children in their new clothes playing with a toy lion's head.

(Take the train to Tai Wai station, or go by taxi). The *Wong Tai Sin* temple is in Kowloon (MTR to Wong Tai Sin then follow the signposts). The Lam Tsuen Valley is best reached by taxi from Tai Po railway station (train from Kowloon terminal).

Establishing the Fortune of the Year

Like the Kitchen God, the God of Wealth has a place in any traditional home. He may be represented by a picture or simply a strip of red paper with his name written on it. On New Year's Eve children go round selling new Wealth God pictures, and on the second day of the New Year the old ones are replaced.

New Year is also the most important period for visiting traditional temples in order to determine the fortune for the new year. Here women usually take the lead. Whichever temple you choose to go to is your own affair. Many people visit several, on the principle that the more *gods* you have to look after you the better. *Wong Tai Sin's* Temple in Kowloon is always exceptionally busy for *Wong Tai Sin* has an excellent reputation for the accuracy of his forecasts and advice.

Another *god* who draws enormous crowds at this time is Ch'e Kung, at his temple in Shatin. A wheel ('ch'e') stands on Ch'e Kung's altar. You give it a turn to symbolize both the cosmic movement of the 'turn' of the year and the hoped for good 'turn' in your own fortune, and then make your offerings. After that you get down to the business of *Asking the Blocks* and *Shaking the Fortune Sticks* to find answers to your questions about the next twelve months.

The *Blocks* — two pieces of wood each convex *(yang)* on one side and flat *(yin)* on the other — look rather like the two halves of a banana split lengthways. To use them, you must first kneel down and ask your question in a form suitable for a 'yes' or 'no' answer. You then drop the *blocks* on the floor and note whether the convex or flat sides are upper-most. One of each ('the holy couple') means that the answer is 'yes'.

The *Fortune Sticks* give a different type of answer. Each *Fortune Stick* is a numbered slip of bamboo kept with many others in a smallish bamboo cylinder. Kneeling, the petitioner shakes the cylinder in such a way that one of the slips falls out. Its number is then checked against a numbered series of written 'fortunes' kept in the temple.

Many traditionally minded people also make New Year expeditions to one of the several sites at which so-called 'nature spirits' are believed to reside. A good example is in the Lam Tsuen Valley in the New Territories where a huge banyan tree is visited at this time by scores of black-clad *Boat Women* from Aberdeen, more than twenty miles away on the far side of Hong Kong island. In the evening when they have left, the tree looks like a strangely off-centre Christmas tree festooned with paper gifts.

Day 15 Yuen Siu, The Lantern Festival

Where to go: There are officially sponsored children's lantern processions which are well advertised in the media. Lantern shows take place at Ko Shan Park (Hung Hom) (bus nos. 116 from Causeway Bay, 101 from Central, 5 from Tsim Sha Tsui, 11 from Jordan Road ferry). Lanterns also dress the *Ancestral Halls* in the New Territories and outlying islands. The New Year is the best time to see the fishing fleet, and the easiest place to see it is at Aberdeen.

The End of the New Year Holiday

In North China the Lantern Festival which marked the end of the New Year period really was a public occasion for lantern processions, masked parades and dragon dances. In Hong Kong more lanterns are seen at the Mid-Autumn Festival in Moon Eight than now, though a rather recent attempt to start an annual children's lantern parade has caught on successfully in the city.

In the villages of the New Territories, however, lanterns are dressed and hung in the *Ancestral Halls* at this time, and any local family to whom a son has been born during the past year brings a lantern to the *Ancestral Hall*. Later, the male members of the clan sit together in the *Ancestral Hall* to eat a special meal. In places like Cheung Chau, on the outlying islands, it is a time of community-wide celebration. Dinners and performances are organized among *K'ai Fong Wooi* (neighbourhood association), *T'ung Heung Wooi* (district association) and *Dzung Tsan Wooi* (clan association).

The return to work after the holidays occurs at various times. In some occupations there is strict control. Fishing boats, for example, must all be moored on New Year's Eve and may not move at all until a selected propitious day and hour after the New Year. Then, on the stroke of the appointed time, all boats move at once — a token move at least. Before setting out to sea again, they are supposed to circle three times in clouds of incense and firecracker smoke. Other occupations have other customs. By the 16th at the very latest, life has returned to normal.

Dressing and preparing the ancestral lantern for Yuen Siu, the Lantern Festival. The same experts do this every year. Peach blossom and New Year cards also appear every year.

A fa p'aau wooi (flowery rocket club) with the fa p'aau, a towering floral shrine, pushes its way through the crowd to pay worship to Hung Shing Kung at his temple on his birthday.

Top left — Details of 'royal' paper robes for offering to the gods. Top right and Bottom left — Close up of one of the royal robes with figures of the Eight Immortals. Bottom right — A warrior's paper robe.

Moon Two

Day 2 Birthday of T'o Tei Kung

Where to go: Nam Pin Wai in Yuen Long (take bus no. 68X from Jordan Road ferry, then taxi), and almost anywhere, especially the villages of the New Territories and the older parts of town.

A God for Every Place

Around sunset every evening throughout the year, the smell of incense draws attention to something easily missed at other times — a tiny shelter or just a cluster of incense sticks on the left hand side of a doorway. Someone has just placed the second of the daily offerings to the T'o Tei Kung there (the first is made at dawn or thereabouts).

One of the oldest *gods*, first mentioned in writing in the year 200 AD but certainly in evidence long before that, he is usually called Earth God or Guardian Spirit in English. However it is necessary to remember that there are literally millions of him, for every single place (neighbourhood, village, house, shop, flat, field...) is supposed to have a T'o Tei Kung to look after it. In return the inhabitants look after their own T'o Tei Kung and make him a little shrine.

Anyone can solicit the resident guardian spirit of his own locality either to keep him informed about what is going on (especially to report a birth or death in his 'patch') or to ask for help in sickness or distress. He is usually friendly and helpful, and the scraps of rag that are sometimes to be seen on sticks near his shrine are votive offerings thanking him for his services.

The second day of the Second Moon (Double Second) is a good day for Earth God spotting, for then the red papers are renewed and new red candles and incense are offered together with little bowls of rice, tea, wine, and perhaps a few oranges. Firecrackers were also offered in the old days.

A brief version of this ceremony happens on the second and sixteenth days of every Moon.

Day 13 Birthday of Hung Shing Kung

Where to go: Offerings are made in all Hung Shing Kung temples on this day. Major celebrations, with operas and *fa p'aau*, are held at Ap Lei Chau (near Aberdeen, taxi or bus no. 90 from Admiralty MTR), Tai O (Lantau, ferry from Outer Islands Pier) and Kau Sai Island (eastern New Territories, bus no. 92, minibus, or taxi to Sai Kung from Choi Hung MTR, then local ferry from water-front). Sha Lo Wan (Lantau, Tai O ferry from Outer Islands pier or Tuen Mun ferry pier) holds a Hung Shing Kung Festival on the 23rd day of the Seventh Moon.

Patron of Seafarers

Hung Shing Kung is venerated by the many thousands of people who make their living on the water and a great many others too.

It is strange that so little is known about so popular a *deity*. One story is that he was a good official in *Kwangtung Province* in the T'ang Dynasty (618–907 AD) who knew how to foretell the weather. Another claims that he is really the Dragon King who rules the Southern Seas. Both stories explain his importance for seafarers, but neither gives many details. However, the lack of legends in no way dampens the ardour of his followers, and his birthday, the first such festival in the year, is enthusiastically celebrated.

A Typical 'Birthday' Festival: Hung Shing Kung on Kau Sai Island

Chinese popular religion gives almost every *deity* a 'birthday' and therefore a birthday party or festival. As the general pattern of all birthday festivals is much the same, the following short description is given here as a model which can be referred to in connection with the stories of other *gods* in later months of the year.

Kau Sai is a tiny fishing village on an otherwise uninhabited island. In 1982 its annual Hung Shing Festival cost somewhere in the region of HK$120,000 most of which was used to pay for a set of nine excellent professional opera performances. The villagers raised the money by subscription amongst themselves and by donations from participants.

About two weeks before the festival opens, a small group of scaffolders arrives to build the so-called *matshed* theatre. On the eleventh day of the Moon the opera troupe arrives. At eight o'clock the curtain goes up. The first short piece is always a ceremonial salute to the birthday *god*. The festival has begun.

Propitiation and Purification

At sundown on the twelfth day a group of *Taoist* priests performs a ritual to purify the village for the ceremonies of the following day and to get rid of any dangerous spirits. It is a short version of the great chiu ceremonies

Day 2
Birthday of
T'o Tei Kung

Day 13
Birthday of
Hung Shing
Kung

Day 19
Birthday of
Koon Yam
(see Moon Nine
day 19)

Also:
Day 2
Birthday of
Mencius

Day 3
Birthday of
Man Ch'eung

Day 15
Birthday of
*Sham Shan
Kwok Wong*

Solar Calendar:
Spring Equinox
(usually 21st
March)

Rockets representing every fa p'aau are shot into the air and members of each fa p'aau club try to grab it, which in turn will bring them good fortune.

which are described under Moon Eleven. After this, hundreds of candles, incense sticks, and bundles of paper clothing and *spirit money* are burned for any predatory ghosts residing on the land and a paper boat, about two feet long, loaded with rice, tea leaves, and paper goods is taken out to sea and set on fire for those on the water.

Later, the priests read aloud a list of all who have contributed to the festival. Then the list, too, is burned on the back of a paper horse and so sent up to Heaven together with the bamboo and paper image of *Taai Si Wong* who has presided over the whole ceremony and will report everything to the *King of Hell* (see Moon Seven). Finally, a copy of the list of names and contributions is posted on the temple wall. Next day is Hung Shing Kung's 'birthday'.

Presentation of Offerings

The festival begins quietly with one or two families coming to the temple before dawn and works up to a climax around mid-day.

The big processions, led by *Dancing Lions* or *Unicorns* belong to *fa p'aau wooi*. The words mean 'flowery rocket club'. Any group of people can join together to make such a club. Each club owns an image of the birthday god, and each member pays a certain sum towards the purchase of the club's offerings and takes part in the procession that carries them to the temple.

The offerings include roast pigs, baskets of oranges, red apples, hard boiled eggs dyed red, roast chicken and pork, and boxes of special buns and cakes. (One year there was a huge Western style birthday cake with yellow icing and the Chinese characters for 'Happy Birthday to Hung Shing Kung' picked out in red.) There are also cups of wine and tea, bunches of red candles, incense sticks, and bundles of paper clothing together with millions of dollars of *spirit money*.

Sometimes a *fa p'aau* club brings more enduring gifts: a new embroidered red silk altar cloth, for example, or a gold medallion to hang round Hung Shing Kung's neck. Such offerings are not burned but left in the temple for its adornment.

First in the procession, after the *Lion*, comes a towering floral shrine. This is the *fa p'aau*. It is made (at the cost of several hundred dollars) of bamboo and coloured paper and hung about with *lettuces* and lumps of *ginger*. The name of the club is written across the top, and on the lower part in a small glass case stands the image of the Saintly Lord Hung.

While the *Dancing Lion* makes obeisance outside the temple, the *fa p'aau* is carefully put down facing the entrance and the club members go inside to place their offerings on the altar, light their candles and incense, burn their paper, and divine their fortunes.

Distribution

Every *fa p'aau* has a number. This is important because after visiting the temple the *fa p'aau* are redistributed among the participating clubs by means of a lucky draw in which the prizes are the *fa p'aau* themselves and — much more importantly — the guarantee of a year's good fortune that goes along with the winning.

The draw takes place in the theatre in the afternoon. First there are speeches, and embroidered banners are presented to the opera stars and local big-wigs who are then invited to draw the lucky numbers of the tickets which have been purchased by dozens of hopeful club members for HK$2 each.

The club with a ticket corresponding to the first number drawn takes *fa p'aau* number 1; the second gets *fa p'aau* number 2; and so on. The luckiest is number 9. It's all very exciting... But less exciting now than it used to be before the law against fireworks was passed in 1967.

In those days, the distribution was done differently, using rockets. As many rockets as there were *fa p'aau* were prepared, each one containing a numbered stick which was shot into the air and then scrambled for by the young champions of each club. Undoubtedly today's raffle is safer. But people's eyes light up when they remember the old days. Rockets are still used at the T'in Hau Festival in Sai Wan, Cheung Chau (15th day of Third Moon) and Sok Kwu Wan, Lamma (beginning of the Fourth Moon) and at the T'o Tei Kung Festival at Tai O, Lantau (23rd day of the First Moon).

After the raffle the clubs collect their *fa p'aau* and members take their individual shares of the food offerings which they will eat later at home. The most important part of the festival is over, though there are still one or two more days and nights of opera before the birthday party comes to its final end.

All major celebrations for *gods'* birthday festivals are more or less like that. The settings vary and there may be different local customs, but the general outlines are the same — variations on a single theme.

Huge 'flower board' is put up at the entrance of the village during the T'o Tei Festival at Nam Pin Wai in Yuen Long.

T'in Hau, Queen of Heaven, Lam Tsuen Temple.

Five Taoists set up an 'invitation and direction post' to call the Hungry Ghosts and feed them with cooked rice, vegetables, and cups of tea and wine. 'Spirit money' is offered as well. Representatives of the villages put on their blue gowns and rattan hats and follow the Taoists at the ceremonies.

集恩堂全人進香
MING LEE
HONG KONG

Moon Three

Ch'ing Ming

Where to go: Ch'ing Ming is observed at all the cemeteries in Hong Kong. The biggest are at Chai Wan, Pokfulam and Aberdeen (bus no. 7 or 70 from Central terminal or taxi), Wo Hop Shek (the biggest) near Fanling, in the New Territories (train to Fanling and taxi or bus no. 70 from Jordan Road ferry, Kowloon, or taxi). Traffic is heavy on these days and public transport crowded.

Spring Remembrance

The words 'Ch'ing Ming' mean 'clear and bright'. This is the time of year when most Chinese go to visit their family graves. The first activity of the visit is to clear away the weeds and repaint the inscriptions (the so-called 'sweeping of the graves'). Then incense sticks and red candles are lighted and rice, wine, tea, and many other foods set out. Paper clothing and *spirit money* are burned and the whole group kneels to pay respects; even the smallest children are gently pressed down and shown how to move their tiny hands up and down — palms together, fingers straight — in the proper gesture of respect to the spirits.

The greetings over, the occasion turns into a family picnic which the living share on the hillsides with their dead. Before they leave they tuck several pieces of offering paper under a stone on top of the grave. They flap a little in the wind, a sign that the grave has been tended for another year.

The occasion is not so very different from the custom of 'dressing the graves' with flowers at Easter which is practised in many parts of the British Isles and by Christians in Hong Kong. Spring time and remembrance seem to go easily together.

Day 3 Birthday of Pak Tai

Where to go: There are several temples to Pak Tai in the city, on both sides of the harbour, at each of which offerings are made on this day. Major celebrations, with operas and *fa p'aau* are held at Stanley (bus nos. 6 or 260 from Central terminal or taxi), on Tsing Yi Island (MTR to Tsuen Wan, then taxi) and Cheung Chau; and in a most attractive and unspoiled setting far out in the north-west corner of the New Territories at Mong Tseng Wai (bus no. 68X from Jordan ferry pier to Yuen Long, then taxi or change to Bus 655 to Lau Fau Shan, then taxi). The Bun Festival on Cheung Chau is also connected with Pak Tai (see Moon Four).

A Legendary Hero

Pak Tai's name means Ruler of the North, but his full title is Superior Divinity of the Deep Dark Heaven, True Soldier of the North.

It is a title linked with myths of times before the dawn of Chinese history when the Demon King was ravaging the Universe and the Great Gods themselves felt bound to intervene. Then the *Primordial Deity* ordered the *Jade Emperor* to appoint Pak Tai commander-in-chief and bade him attack the Demons.

Dressed in a black robe and with a golden breast-plate, Pak Tai fought barefoot, his long hair flowing over his shoulders. Needless to say he overcame the Demon King and all his evil hosts (including a magical serpent and tortoise which he had conjured up to his aid) and returned victorious, to be awarded an even grander title: First Lord of Heaven.

The vanquished snake and tortoise are faithfully reproduced on all Pak Tai's images in Hong Kong. So are the bare feet. But it is interesting to note that a tortoise is in any case the accepted (and very ancient) Chinese symbol for the North. So is the colour black.

Day 3
Birthday of
Pak Tai

Day 23
Birthday of
T'in Hau

Also:
Day 15
Birthday of
Po Sheng Ta Tai

Solar Calendar:
Ch'ing Ming
(usually 5 or 6
April, may be in
Moon Two)

Day 23 Birthday of T'in Hau

Where to go: T'in Hau, Queen of Heaven, has more than forty temples dedicated to her in Hong Kong. All are busy on this day, and at least twenty-four of them are scenes of major celebration. Since it would be impossible to find enough actors in Hong Kong to stage twenty-four separate sets of operas at the same time, some of these festivals are staggered. Here is a selected list:

Date of the Main Day of Festival	Place	Special Features
15th day of 3rd moon	Sai Wan, Cheung Chau (ferry from Outer Islands pier)	Many *fa p'aau*; rocket competition (see p. 30 above).
23rd day of 3rd moon	Joss House Bay (special ferries from North Point pier)	Huge fleet of harbour *Boat People*. No opera.
23rd day of 3rd moon	Yuen Long (bus no. 68X from Jordan Rd. ferry, Kowloon, or taxi)	Giant parade in sports stadium; more than 40 *fa p'aau* clubs.

Approaching the big T'in Hau Temple in Joss House Bay for T'in Hau's birthday festival, 23rd day of Moon Three.

Date of the Main Day of Festival	Place	Special Features
23rd day of 3rd moon	Ping Che (bus no. 79K from Sheung Shui KCR)	Many *fa p'aau*; excellent opera, both Cantonese and *Ch'iu Chau.*
23rd day of 3rd moon every other year (even numbers)	Leung Shuen Wan (High Island) (bus no. 92, minibus, or taxi to Sai Kung from Choi Hung MTR, then local ferry)	Goddess is paraded at sea on 22nd day; interesting Chiu ceremonies that evening.
25th day of 4th moon	Tsing Yi Island (MTR to Tsuen Wan, then taxi)	More than 100 *fa p'aau* in competition.
Beginning of 4th moon (date varies)	Sai Kung (MTR to Choi Hung, then bus no. 92 or minibus no. 1, or taxi.)	Excellent opera, both Cantonese and *Ch'iu Chau*
Beginning of 4th moon (date varies)	Sok Kwu Wan, Lamma Island (ferry from Outer Islands pier).	Many *fa p'aau*; rocket competition (see p. 30 above)

Miss Lin the Fisherman's Daughter

On the 23rd day of the Third Moon in a certain year in the tenth century AD a red light was seen descending upon the house of a poor fisherman named Lin who lived on a small island off the coast of Fukien Province, about 300 miles up the coast from Hong Kong. Soon afterwards a baby girl was born there.

She was a most unusual baby who never cried and even in her childhood showed many signs of holiness. One day, she dreamed that she saw her father and two brothers on two junks in the midst of a terrible storm. She immediately grasped the two boats by their rigging and started to pull them ashore. At that very moment, her mother shook her by the arm to wake her up and caused her to let go of one set of ropes. Later when her two brothers returned home, they described how a beautiful girl had walked across the raging waters and dragged their boat to safety but had been unable to save their father too.

After her death, still unmarried, at the early age of 28, story after story began to be told by sailors to whom she had appeared in stormy weather and saved from almost certain death. The red light of her birth was often seen upon the mast-head (St Elmo's Fire, as Western sailors call this phenomenon) and greeted as a sign of her protection — 'Our Mother's Fire'.

Very soon almost every ship was carrying an image of Miss Lin, and temples dedicated to her began to be built up and down the coasts of Fukien and *Kwangtung*.

Her Canonisation

After two centuries of popular veneration, Miss Lin was officially canonised in the twelfth century and given the title Saintly and Diligent Saviour. She subsequently received a series of increasingly exalted titles and sometime before the middle of the fifteenth century was awarded a place among the stars of the Great Bear (in *Taoist* thinking the most important of the constellations). Finally in 1683 after having assisted the Imperial Chinese Fleet in the re-conquest of Taiwan, she was promoted Queen of Heaven (T'in Hau).

It is not difficult to understand the popularity of such a *goddess* among the hundreds of thousands who sail the proverbially unpredictable South China Sea and the many others in a great commercial port like Hong Kong who owe their livelihood to shipping. The fact that she is of relatively local origin probably also speaks in her favour. In many ways like Kwan Yin, she is also regarded as the special protector of women and children. To most believers she is known quite simply as 'Mother'.

Cantonese comedy.

Hillside graves: the main cemetery at Wo Hop Shek in the New Territories. On the day of the Ch'ing Ming Festival, people jostle their way to pay homage to their ancestors and deceased relatives.

Top left — Caring for ancestors: 'golden pagodas' contain ancestral bones. Bottom left — Flowers for the Christian dead; a Ch'ing Ming visit to the Roman Catholic cemetery in Happy Valley. Top right — Clan offerings to the ancestors. Bottom right — Ancestral bones are carefully stowed in their 'golden pagodas'.

明三世祖
妣李氏孺人之墓

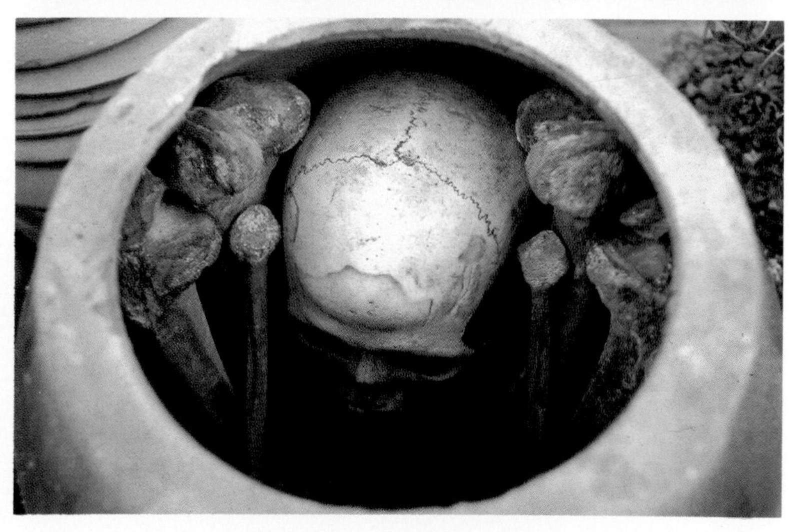

吸煙
煙

Moon Four

Day 8 Birthday of the Lord Buddha

The Founder of Buddhism

Prince Siddhartha Sakyamuni, founder of *Buddhism*, was born in the sixth century BC in a small state in what is now the kingdom of Nepal.

His father, the king, determined to keep him at home, surrounded him with luxury and tried to prevent him from seeing any sad or ugly sights. On four occasions, however, he failed.

On the first occasion, the boy happened to see the pain of extreme old age; on the second, he encountered a man who was seriously ill; on the third he saw a funeral. Tortured by these sights, Sakyamuni began to ask the age-old question: Why?

The fourth occasion changed his life. One day he met a poor monk begging for food. Despite the monk's poverty, he had a look of great happiness. Surprised by this, the prince dismounted from his horse and talked with him for a long time. That very night he left the palace secretly and began the life of a wandering mendicant, resolved, like the monk, to seek the truth.

After six years in which he experienced the most severe privations, he sat down under a peepul tree to meditate, declaring that he would not rise until he had found the answer to the riddle of suffering. At first — rather like Jesus in the wilderness — Sakyamuni was grievously tempted by Mara, the Spirit of Evil, who sent demons to try to terrify him and then his own beautiful daughters to seduce him. Finally, Mara admitted defeat and, while all the hosts of Heaven rejoiced, Gautama (as he was now more usually called) received the Ultimate Peace of True Knowledge.

The rest of his long life (he was 35 when he attained enlightenment and 79 when he died) was spent in preaching this Truth to others. His message was simple to understand but hard to follow: all human misery is caused by the fact that people are too much attached to the world. What one must do, therefore, is renounce all desire. Detach yourself from all the manifestations of selfhood and you will attain peace.

Buddhist Institutions and Ceremonial Activities

In China, as elsewhere, *Buddhism* is based on the monastic life, but there are also groups of laymen and women who vow to follow the Buddha's precepts in the world and perhaps go into retreat from time to time. In addition, there is an unknown multitude of individual believers.

The major temples and monasteries in Hong Kong are at Castle Peak, at Shatin and on Lantau Island; there are many smaller ones. *Buddhists* also run charitable organizations such as schools, old people's homes, clinics, and a hospital.

All *Buddhist* temples hold ceremonies on Buddha's birthday and on the anniversaries of his enlightenment — on the 8th day of the Ninth Moon, and death — on the 8th day of the Second Moon. The Buddhist Association of Hong Kong also arranges major ceremonies. (Apply in writing to the Secretary for further information.)

Day 8 Birthday of T'am Kung

Where to go: Taxi, bus no. 20 from Central bus terminus, tram or MTR to Shau Kei Wan at the eastern end of Hong Kong Island. Walk straight down Main Street East. The crowds will lead you to the temple.

Insurance against Fire, Flood and Tempest

T'am Kung is another of the *deities* whose appeal is largely (though certainly not exclusively) to people who live and work on boats. He specializes in weather control. By throwing up a handful of peas he can calm the most violent storm, or, alternatively, by substituting a cup of water for the peas he can cause a downpour heavy enough to put out a fire.

It is not surprising, therefore, that he has a staunch following among the lightermen of the harbour whose livelihood still depends greatly upon the weather and for whom a fire on board can spell disaster. Anyone who lives in the older, most combustible parts of the city, or in the squatter settlements, is also likely to consider that an offering to T'am Kung may be a useful form of insurance. Besides quelling storms, T'am Kung can also heal the sick by influencing their subconscious minds while they are asleep.

His festival, a *god's* birthday party of the type described under Moon Two, is one of Hong Kong Island's most spectacular celebrations.

Day 8
Birthday of the
Lord Buddha

Day 8
Birthday of
T'am Kung

Day varies
Cheung Chau
Bun Festival
(date selected
annually by
divination)

Also:
Day 14
Birthday of
Lu Tung-pin

Day 17
Birthday of
Kam Fa

Day 18
Birthday of
Wah T'oh

Mountains of Buns: the foothills of the three great 'peaks' at Cheung Chau. People prepare the Bun Mountains and the three huge effigies before the Festival begins.

Day varies: Cheung Chau Bun Festival

Where to go: Take any Cheung Chau ferry from the Outer Islands piers (about ten minutes walk westward from the Hong Kong Star Ferry). The journey takes about 50 minutes. It is advisable to start early and be prepared for a long, hot, but quite unparalleled day.

Dates: The Bun Festival lasts for six days in all, during two nights and three days only vegetarian food is available on the island. The dates are not fixed but selected each year by the god Pak Tai himself (see Moon Three) through divination. His choice, which is nearly always early in Moon Four, is well publicized in the media and by the Hong Kong Tourist Association.

Mountains of Buns

The central features of this festival are three huge conical bamboo and paper towers — about sixty feet tall — each one covered all over with layer upon layer of pink and white buns. Each bun is a part of the grand offering to the *ghosts* which is one of the main purposes of the festival, and also a symbol of good fortune and a talisman against sickness for whoever is lucky enough to obtain it.

The towers dominate the festival and the distribution of the buns at midnight on the last night is the climax towards which everything moves. At midnight, after the *ghosts* have had their fill of the spiritual essence of the buns, the congregation is invited to scramble for the material remains. A concerted rush by all the young men present carries some right to the top and leaves others spread-eagled across the surface of the towers, stripping buns as fast as they can. In about three and a half minutes there is nothing left but scaffolding and torn paper. The festival is over for another year. Or... that is how it used to be.

In 1977, however, one of the bun towers collapsed under the assault. No one was seriously hurt (many islanders pointed out that of course Pak Tai would not have allowed such a thing to happen) but since then the scramble has been officially forbidden. Instead, the buns are distributed by hand the next morning to patient queues of mainly women and children.

Processions Galore

But the people of Cheung Chau are not content merely to placate their *ghosts*; they also want to commemorate an occasion about one hundred years ago when an outbreak of plague on the island was finally wiped out after Pak Tai's image had been paraded through the streets. In honour of that event the whole small town is *en fête*, two opera troupes are engaged to perform in a vast matshed theatre opposite Pak Tai's temple. The Cantonese opera performs before the processions and the *Hoklo* opera after the processions. The processions are of a kind that can be seen nowhere else in Hong Kong and are carried out on the last two days.

The main attractions in the processions are children usually between the ages of five and eight who are carried shoulder high through the narrow streets. Each child represents a figure in history, romance, or mythology, and each is meticulously made up and dressed for the part. But the most striking thing is the way in which these small actors, posed above the heads of the crowd, appear to be performing impossible feats of balance, all under perfect control and apparently in complete comfort.

The procession includes the usual *Dancing Lions* and *Unicorns* with their drummers, *kung fu* clubs with their banners, adult actors impersonating well-known story figures, and, of course, a band.

At the front of the procession, leading the way, come eight red sedan chairs with portable images of the chief *deities* from all the temples on the island — Pak Tai, Hung Shing Kung, three T'in Haus, Koon Yam, Kwan Tai, and, finally, a second Pak Tai under his title Superior Ruler of Primordial Heaven. As the head of the procession nears the temple, the chair carriers break away and race to the door: Is the winner always Pak Tai?

Bun Festival. Most of the rites are performed at the Taoist matshed but some at various other locations. This ceremony is performed in front of the temporary temple of the gods; it must be performed at the chosen time, regardless of the weather.

The Cheung Chau Bun Festival begins with the Taoist rites 'Inviting the Gods'.

Musicians: the Sonaat player, the Gong player, the Yi Wu player, and the paper sculptor who puts finishing touches to Taai Si Wong are all major participants in the festivals.

'Mo si', Dancing Lion, one of the many performances during the procession of the Cheung Chau Bun Festival. The lion shown here is known as the lion of the north, usually identified by its distinctive orange mane.

The Float Procession during the Bun Festival. The children are dressed to represent people in history, romance, mythology or even television drama. They are supported on frames and carried shoulder high throughout the parade.

Mobil

Moon Five

Day 5 Dragon Boat Races

Where to go: The Dragon Boats appear about a month before the Festival when the crews start training. The easiest places to see them are Stanley, Shau Kei Wan, Aberdeen, and Chai Wan on Hong Kong Island; or near Tai Po or Sai Kung in the New Territories. On the Double Fifth, officially sponsored races are organized at various places including Aberdeen (bus no. 70 from Central terminal or taxi), Yau Ma Tei (Kowloon MTR Yau Ma Tei station) and Sai Kung (eastern New Territories: bus no. 92, minibus no. 1, or taxi from MTR station at Choi Hung). They are all well advertised in the media. The International Dragon Boat Race meeting is usually held on a Saturday after the 5th.

Chinese Dragons

The most important thing to remember about Chinese dragons is that they are entirely beneficent creatures. Thus while a Western hero (like Saint George) might be awarded the title, 'dragon killer', a Chinese hero was more likely to be called a 'dragon' himself, like the Emperor who sat on the Dragon Throne.

The Chinese dragons are purely mythical beasts made up of a marvellous mixture of other animals, including the head of a camel, the horns of a deer, eyes of a hare, ears of a cow, neck of a snake, belly of a frog, scales of a carp, claws of a hawk, and paws of a tiger. Their backs are crested, their mouths are decorated with whiskers, and the beard of each hides a shining pearl.

The Boats

However, the Dragon Boat dragons are mainly head and tail, the body being a long, narrow canoe-like boat, with seats for the paddlers to sit two abreast. The heads and tails, which are detachable, are kept for the rest of the year in local temples and new heads must always be properly dedicated in a ceremony called '*opening the light*'. This involves painting each eye with a dot of vermilion paint mixed with blood from the comb of a brown chicken. Once this has been done, the dragon is 'alive' and has to be treated with ceremonious respect, presented with incense and candles, and protected from anything that might endanger its essentially *Yang* character, such as contact with women. (Nowadays women do have a place in the official races, but their boats are *Phoenixes*, not *Dragons*).

The biggest Dragon Boats are up to a hundred feet in length and cost between about HK$80,000 and HK$100,000 at today's prices. They are built in such a way that they can travel tail first as easily as head first, which is just as well since their length makes it much easier for the crew to turn themselves round rather than the boat. There may be as many as fifty paddlers, a drummer to keep the time, and an oarsman who stands at the stern and steers.

Each boat belongs to a certain locality or association and competition is usually intense. The winners in the main events are nearly always fishermen.

Legendary History

Every year on this day newspapers in Hong Kong tell the story of *Wat Yuen* who lived historically in the third century BC when China was still divided among a number of small kingdoms known as the Warring States.

Minister to the king of one of these states, *Wat Yuen* was also one of China's greatest poets. He did his best to advise the king wisely, but his advice was rejected and he was dismissed from his post. Leaving the court in despair, he wandered along beside the river and there sat down to compose his most beautiful poem. It was a summary of his life, a statement of his ideals, and a formal farewell to his country. Then he threw himself into the river.

The people of that district took to their boats to search for him and when they realized he was drowned they threw rice into the water in the hope that the fishes thereabouts would eat that and spare his body. So, we are told, in commemoration of this sad event, the Dragon Boats race about on the water every year as if looking for *Wat Yuen* and everyone eats dumplings of sticky rice wrapped up in leaves.

Wat Yuen was indeed a historical figure and one of China's greatest poets whose works are still widely read, but it seems that the picturesque tale of the search for his body was an invention of a later date. In any case, this popular story does nothing to explain the size of the great canoes and why they have dragons' heads and tails.

A Widespread Southeast Asian Custom?

A different kind of explanation is suggested by the fact that although the Double Fifth is an important festival all over the country, it is only in Central China and the South that it is celebrated with Dragon Boat races.

Day 5
Dragon Boat
Festival

Day 13
Birthday of
Kwan Tai

Also:
Day 8
Birthday of the
Dragon Mother

Day 18
Birthday of
the *Master of Heaven*
(*Cheung T'in Si*)

Solar Calendar:
Summer Solstice
(usually 21st
June)

Officially sponsored dragon boat races.

It is known that when *Wat Yuen* was alive very few Chinese lived in the South. The large majority of the people there at that time were non-Chinese tribal groups related to the modern populations of the countries of South East Asia.

It is interesting to note that most contemporary South East Asian countries hold elaborate water festivals in the spring and early summer, some of which include river parades and races between long canoe-like boats with animal heads and tails. This makes one wonder whether there is some connection between today's Dragon Boats in Hong Kong and more widespread non-Chinese customs of long ago.

The Benevolent Power of Chinese Dragons and the Dangerous Double Fifth

Whether or not there is any such connection, it is certain that the Dragon symbol is essentially Chinese, and so is the choice of date for the festival.

There is a widespread idea that the Dragon Boat races have something to do with fertility. This may be connected with the fact that the Fifth Moon is in the growing season when the crops require rain, and because dragons live in water or the clouds they are supposed to be able to bring rain. In Hong Kong rain usually falls during or soon after the Dragon Boat Festival every year.

The benevolent power of the Dragon Boats is also believed to be useful in the cure and prevention of disease. In the words of one Roman Catholic fisherman in Aberdeen in 1953: 'Even though I'm too old now to take part in the races, I always have a turn or two at paddling the Dragon Boat to protect my family from sickness.'

Perhaps because it is the first really hot month of the year and the one in which the *Yang* powers are at their height with the approach of the Summer Solstice, the Fifth Moon is traditionally believed to be the period in which disease is most prevalent and all kinds of other dangers abound. The most dangerous day of all is the Double Fifth, so it is not surprising that the prophylactic Dragon Boat races should be held on that day. However, it seems that the Dragon Boats alone are not enough; many other charms are also brought out at this time for extra insurance. Even the Dragon Boats themselves need protection. They are hung about with the pointed leaves of iris and certain grasses while at the same time bunches of the common mugwort (artemisia vulgaris) or other aromatic leaves are dangled over the doors of village houses, often with a piece of pork and perhaps an onion.

The pointed leaves represent demon-slaying swords; the pork is a left over bit of temple offering charged with heavenly potency; and the belief in the power of strong scents to ward off evil is as strong as it is widespread. (Mugwort was a well-known charm in ancient Greece and was used against sorcery all over Europe not so long ago. Some English country people still put half a raw onion on a saucer in the corner of the bedroom to cure a cold.)

Day 13 Birthday of Kwan Tai

Where to go: In addition to being God of War and Literature, Kwan Tai is the patron of pawnshops, restaurants and many other merchants, as well as the police. There are always a great many private celebrations of his birthday today, but most outsiders will have to be content with just noticing that they are happening. (Be warned, however, the date of Kwan Tai's anniversary is disputed and some groups celebrate on the 24th day of Moon Six instead.)

Everybody's Hero

Model of loyalty and courage, perfect incarnation of the spirit of chivalry, impetuous, commanding, and immensely strong, Kwan Tai was a hero of the period of chaos that followed the collapse of the great Han Dynasty in 220 AD. For a Western festival watcher he is perhaps best introduced as a kind of blend of King Arthur, Robin Hood, and Frederick Barbarossa. He had a massive sword called Green Dragon that outshines the moon, and a matchless horse, Red Hare.

His story is written with loving detail in the most famous of all Chinese novels *The Romance of the Three Kingdoms*, reproduced a thousand times in the plots of Chinese operas, repeated for centuries by story tellers, and today summarized over and over again in strip cartoons. Every Chinese child used to be brought up on these tales. A serious festival watcher will want to read them too. The reading list will help to find the books.

Dragon boat races in Tai O, Lantau.

A Tanka (boat people) woman tries to divine the future by shaking a fortune stick out of a bamboo cylinder.

Paper image of Koon Yam standing next to Taai Si Wong at the Hungry Ghosts Festival, in Shatin. Taai Si Wong is a manifestation of Koon Yam.

Moon Six

Day 6 Birthday of Hau Wong

Where to go: Celebrations are held at Hau Wong Temple near Kowloon City (taxi or bus no. 1A from the Star Ferry, Tsim Sha Tsui, or nos. 101, 111 from Central bus terminus) and at Tai O (Lantau). At Tung Chung (Lantau) the Hau Wong festival is held on the 16th day of the Eighth month. (Tai O can be reached by ferry from the Outlying Islands ferry pier or Tuen Mun ferry bay; Tung Chung by bus no. 3 from Silvermine Bay, or by kaido [small boat] from Castle Peak Bay).

The Sung Emperor in Hong Kong

The story of Hau Wong dates from the latter part of the thirteenth century AD when the last Emperor of the Sung Dynasty, fleeing by sea from the victorious Mongols, landed briefly near what is now Kowloon.

The Emperor, who was only an eight-year-old boy, had a devoted bodyguard whose leader, named Yeung, had been taken seriously ill. When the court left on the last stage of the journey which was to lead to the Emperor's death by drowning (suicide being more honourable than surrender), Yeung was left behind to organize defence against possible pursuit.

Unfortunately his illness was too advanced and he died, but not before he had endeared himself to the local people for his honesty, loyalty, and courage in adversity. He was given the posthumous title of Hau Wong (Price Marquis), and in 1731 a temple was built to his memory near the then walled city of Kowloon.

Before the Second World War this was one of the most popular local temples, but since then its prestige has declined and the big festival processions of former years are no longer held. However, the temple is still usually quite well attended and is well worth a visit.

There are two other Hau Wong Temples, at Tai O and Tung Chung, both on Lantau Island at places which were once fortified. The temple at Tung Chung is some distance from the village on an open grassy site near the sea. The festival here is one of the few at which there is enough space to see everything without difficulty. It should be noted, however, that it takes place in the Eighth Moon, not the Sixth.

Day 13 Birthday of Lu Pan

Where to go: Lu Pan's temple is in Kennedy Town at the western end of Hong Kong Island. It is easily reached from the terminus of the no. 23 bus in Pokfulam. From the bus terminus, cross over the road and walk back towards the city until you reach the entrance to a flight of steps named Precious Dragon Terrace. The temple is on the third terrace down (Green Lotus Terrace) next door to a Chinese Middle School.

Patron Saint of Carpenters and Builders

Lu Pan is said to have been born in 606 BC, the son of a man named Pan who lived in the ancient kingdom of Lu in modern Shantung Province. Hence his name.

By the time he was 40, Lu Pan had become the most highly skilled carpenter of his day. He then took up the study of *Taoist* alchemy at which he was so successful that he quickly gained the reputation of having miraculous powers.

His many remarkable accomplishments included repairing the Pillars of Heaven when they were in danger of collapse and building a palace for the *Queen Mother of the Western Heaven*. He anticipated the machine age by making a wooden carriage for his mother which moved by itself and a wooden kite on which he was able to travel through the air.

A *Taoist Immortal*, Lu Pan did not die but simply vanished skywards, leaving behind his axe and saw. His practical advice remains available for any architect or construction worker who needs it, and whenever a new building is begun a feast is spread for him, complete with candles, incense, and the burning of *spirit money*.

Before the Second World War the carpenters of Canton were famous for their splendid processions in honour of Lu Pan's birthday. These no longer occur, but in Hong Kong representatives of the building and carpentry trades pay their respects in his temple at noon, and the evening sees hundreds of celebration dinners in restaurants all over the city.

Day 19 The Enlightenment of Koon Yam

Where to go: The *Boat People* and ex-*Boat People* of Pak Sha Wan (Hebe Haven) hold a *god's* birthday festival for Koon Yam at this time, with operas and *fa p'aau*. The small temple stands between two shops just opposite the entrance to the pier. (Taxi, or bus no. 92 or minibus from the MTR station at Choi Hung). For further details about Koon Yam see Moon Nine.

Day 6
Birthday of
Hau Wong

Day 13
Birthday of
Lu Pan

Day 19
Enlightenment
of Koon Yam

Bundles of incense are offered inside T'in Hau Temple, Lam Tsuen.

Finishing touches for Taai Si Wong inside the temple. The colourful paper sculpture often attracts the children living around. T'in Hau Temple, Tap Mun.

Top left — Taai Si Wong's note book in which he records all the names of the ghosts and potential trouble-makers in the area. Top right — Taai Si Wong's henchmen with chains and staves for punishing unruly ghosts. Bottom right — City God officiating at the On Lung ceremonies. Bottom left — T'o Tei Kung waits for the 'Opening Light Ceremony' which will unbandage his eyes.

雲來集菩薩摩訶薩
切以牛頭象藏龍腦麝涎氤氳法界壇
中馥郁毘耶室內結祥雲而作蓋凝瑞
氣以爲臺泥蓮岸邊與法身而齊長
闍維會理共金骨以俱成六銖可換
於千金一炷能熏於三際教外別傳
之旨當體全彰刦前未照之機通身
顯露我今此一瓣香信手拈來熱向
寶爐願聖遙聞普同供養
聞思脩入三摩地
戒定熏成五分香

Moon Seven

Day 7 Festival of the Seven Sisters

Where to go: This festival is celebrated at home, but it is well worth taking a walk through the older residential parts of the city where many small groups display their offerings and perform simple ceremonies out of doors.

The Cowherd and the Weaving Girl

Once upon a time, while the seven daughters of the Jade Emperor were bathing, a passing Cowherd stole one of their piles of clothing and ran off with it to his house. When the seven sisters came out of the river, the prettiest one was dreadfully embarrassed to discover that before she could get dressed she had to go and ask the Cowherd for her clothes.

Now, of course, once a man had seen her naked, the only possible thing for her to do was to marry him. So she did and for three years they lived happily together. At the end of that time, however, the *gods* ordered the girl back to Heaven to get on with her job of weaving their robes. All that the lovers were allowed was one glimpse of each other a year.

Eventually the Cowherd died. With the help of his magic Cow he became an *Immortal* and made haste to join his beloved among the stars. But before he could reach her, the Queen of Heaven, who feared that her wardrobe might be depleted again, took out her magic hairpin and, with one sweep of her arm, drew the Milky Way across the sky leaving the Cowherd on one side and the Weaving Girl on the other.

There they remain to this day, within sight of one another yet quite unable to communicate except once a year, on the Double Seventh. On that day all the magpies in the world fly up to Heaven and make a bridge with their wings for the Weaving Girl to cross over to visit her husband.

The Maidens' Festival

This story is annually remembered by young unmarried girls who make offerings to the lovers and look into the future to discover when they will marry and whom.

Though the offerings vary in size and quality, they are all of a similar design: a circular tray (made of paper and card) with a picture in the middle. The Weaving Girl is shown standing on a bridge over a stream where the Cowherd and his Cow are wading. In the background are her six sisters. Around the edge of the tray are the various items the seven sisters need for their toilet: seven combs, seven mirrors, seven powder puffs, and so on, and enough paper flowers for them all to put in their hair. In addition, paper clothes and other gifts are also set out for the couple.

The considerable expense of the more elaborate displays is usually met by a group of girls clubbing together (like sisters) and contributing so much a month out of their earnings. It is interesting that modernization, which has given young women the previously unheard of opportunity of earning their own living, has given an extra lease of life to this picturesque festival.

Day 15 Yuen Laan or The Festival for the Hungry Ghosts

Where to go: This festival is widely observed and, since most of the more spectacular ceremonies occur in town, they are easily accessible. Dates and places vary a little from year to year, but the festivals are not difficult to find; just look for the *matshed* theatres and go there. There is usually a conspicuous one opposite the railway station at Shatin in the New Territories.

Ancestors and Ghosts

The Chinese language makes a clear distinction between *ancestors* and *ghosts*. *Ancestors* are 'tso sin', a term which could be translated 'former holy founders', the others are simply 'kwai' — disembodied spirits, *ghosts*. There are vast numbers of *ghosts*.

Some died without children; others were unlucky enough to have all their descendants die out; still others have been unable to reach the world of the dead because they had no proper funeral. All these are the underprivileged dead. They get none of the food, paper clothing, and *spirit money* that are showered upon *ancestors*, and none of their great respect. And they resent it. That is why they are dangerous.

By no means everyone believes in *ghosts*, but for those who do the Seventh Moon is a particularly worrying time. Then the gates of the underworld are opened, and the *ghosts* are free to roam wherever they like.

It is therefore necessary to placate them by offering the same gifts that are normally given to *ancestors* and *gods*. It is also wise to entertain them with several nights and days of opera.

Day 7
Ts'at Tse Mooi:
Seven Sisters' Festival

Day 15
Yue Laan or
Hungry Ghosts Festival

Also:
Day 1
Birthday of *Ts'oi Pak Shing Kwan*

Day 24
Birthday of *City God*

Day 30
Birthday of *Tei Chong Wong*

Buddhist liturgical texts seen at the Hungry Ghosts Festival in Shatin.

Community Celebrations

No other festival in the year produces more large scale community celebrations than this one.

Each set of celebrations is housed in temporary *matshed* constructions built round a playground or other open space. On one side is the theatre. Opposite it is a longish table, or altar, where huge sticks of incense are burning night and day. A constant stream of worshippers comes here to kneel, pray, and place fresh incense sticks. Most of them are women. From time to time *Buddhist* monks and *Taoist* priests come in turns to chant their liturgies.

Behind the altar is the temporary temple, to which images representing the *deities* of the various local temples have been carried in sedan chairs. On one side of the shrine is the organizing committee's busy office, rigged up with telephones, typewriters, and so on, and a big collecting box. Usually the third and fourth sides of the quadrangle are occupied by the temporary headquarters of the *Taoist* and *Buddhist* officiants and by lavish displays of the offerings together with the towering paper figure of *Taai Si Wong* with his attendants.

Taai Si Wong

The climax of each festival is the sending of food, paper clothing, and *spirit money* to the hungry *ghosts*. Except for the food, which is distributed later, everything else is burned. This is always late on the last evening. At the very end, the gigantic paper figure of *Taai Si Wong* is carried from one end of the bonfire to the other and back again so that he can check that everything has been properly completed. Assured, he too returns to Hell in Flames.

Who, then is *Taai Si Wong*? You cannot fail to notice him. Fifteen feet, perhaps, in height with a notebook in his left hand and a pen in his right hand, he dominates the whole proceedings. He is both policeman and recorder, watching everything, writing it down, and reporting later to the King of Hell. At least, that is one story.

If you look closely, however, you will notice that somewhere on or near the figure of *Taai Si Wong* there is a small Koon Yam. Some people say that the person who first gave a feast for the *hungry ghosts* was kind Koon Yam, Goddess of Mercy, but when the *ghost* guests came they behaved so badly that next time she decided to ask the King of Hell to help her keep order. And all the *ghosts* have behaved very nicely ever since. He was said by some to be a mountain *ghost* who had come under the spell of Koon Yam and was made to help her suppress evil *ghosts* by eating them. Some believes that he is the reincarnation of *Yim Lo Wong*.

Other people give yet another explanation. They say that Koon Yam can appear in many different forms. Fundamentally she is always the same loving *Boddhisatva*, but sometimes it is necessary for her to appear to be fierce. According to this view, then, *Taai Si Wong* or *Yim Lo Wong* is just Koon Yam herself in another manifestation.

Lesser Ceremonies: Shiu Yi

In addition to the big communal ceremonies many smaller ones are performed during the first two weeks of this moon when private families, street associations, and other clubs make their own offerings to the *ghosts*. The short name for all these ceremonies, '*shiu yi*', means 'burning clothes'. You are likely to see many of them in the streets at night.

Sometime during this Moon you may also notice gaily decorated lighters circulating the harbour. These are taking offerings to the many *ghosts* who died at sea during the war or in typhoons. The boats make a complete tour of the harbour area, while *Buddhist* monks or *Taoist* priests chant their liturgies on board and pious believers — mostly women — scatter rice upon the water and now and then launch gift-filled paper boats.

Many villages also hold a small '*shiu yi*' ceremony on the 14th, 15th or 16th day. The elders first go to the temple or *ancestral hall* to inform the *gods* and *ancestors*. Then on the open space outside they burn incense, paper clothing, and lots of *spirit money* for the *ghosts*. If it is a seaside village they also fill a paper boat with paper goods and food and launch it, burning, out to sea.

Then comes the part the children like. Among the offerings there are always sweets and fruit. Once the *ghosts* have had their spiritual fill, the Headman gives a shout and all the children come running to scramble for what is left.

This fifteen-foot Taai Si Wong is a popular image at most of the festivals. He is a fierce colossus constructed on a bamboo frame covered in coloured paper and foil, with a papier-mâché head. Before the festival begins, the paper sculptor assembles the parts of Taai Si Wong and erects him in front of the temple.

Preparing food for feeding the Hungry Ghosts who died at sea.

Facing page: Food for the Hungry Ghosts. Top two — Noodles. Bottom right — Buns. Bottom left — Dishes of sweet dumplings and sauce.

新潮利麵廠
敬喜

The monk in his ritual crown during the Hungry Ghosts Festival.

The Chairman of the organizing committee of the Shatin Yue Laan Festival makes his worship as the monks chant around him.

Monks chant the Yue Laan liturgy, regardless of a woman worshipper kneeling in deep trance.

Monks worshipping in front of the Taai Si Wong during the Hungry Ghosts Festival.

記
料

Moon Eight

Day 15 Mid-Autumn Festival (also known as the Moon Festival)

Where to go: From about 7.00 pm onwards Victoria Park in Causeway Bay, Repulse Bay, Stanley Beach, the Peak, and many other open spaces present a charming scene of family parties picnicking quietly on the ground, surrounded by lighted candles and small lanterns. Religious papershops all over Hong Kong have paper lanterns for sale at this season. Moon cakes are available from bakeries, supermarkets, stores, and some restaurants from about the end of August. There are officially organized 'carnivals' and Lantern shows. These will be well publicized.

Enjoying the Moon

The full moon of the Mid-Autumn festival and the Harvest Moon of Europe are the same, and the Harvest suppers of the old agricultural year in England took place at much the same time as the family parties for eating moon cakes and watching the moon in China.

In traditional China the Mid-Autumn festival was especially a woman's occasion, befitting the essentially female *(Yin)* moon. In each family a special table was set up facing the moon out of doors with dishes of round fruit (round for the fullness of the moon) such as apples, oranges, peaches, or pomegranates (the last being particularly propitious since their many seeds symbolize many sons) and, of course, moon cakes. Rice, wine and tea would be offered too, together with several suits of paper clothing and many ingots of *spirit money* in gold and silver paper.

Today these rites are less commonly performed, but the evening is still marked by a family dinner at home. In recent years it has become the custom to take the young children to the nearest park after dinner and settle down with them on the ground to light small candles, nibble moon cakes, and enjoy the moon. Wealthier families often hold moon parties on this date.

Day 16 Monkey's Festival at Sau Mau Ping

Where to go: The festival described here is held in one of the big low-cost housing estates near Kwun Tong, Kowloon. It is not easy to find and for visitors a taxi is recommended. (Show the driver the address given in Chinese in the Glossary under *Sau Mau Ping*.)

The Universal Trickster: Great Sage Equal to Heaven

In Chinese legends, Monkey holds much the same place as Puck or Robin Goodfellow in England, Brer Rabbit in the new world, and many others. He is the naughty, cheeky fellow who successfully takes on the Establishment, whether human or divine, and (often) gets away with it.

His exploits are recounted in a long saga called *The Journey to the West*, which describes the adventures of the monk, *Yuen Tsong*, who was sent to India to fetch the *Buddhist* scriptures.

Yuen Tsong was a historical person in the T'ang Dynasty (618–907 AD) and the epic journey was really made. Around it grew an enormous collection of legendary tales in which *Yuen Tsong* is aided by an assortment of supernatural creatures under the general superintendence of the Lord Buddha through Koon Yam. Dominating this motley group was the scaramouche Monkey who, having previously stormed into Heaven itself and stolen the Peaches of Immortality, had made himself indestructible and acquired miraculous powers. He possessed a magic iron weapon small enough to tuck behind his ear which could in a twinkling become a massive cudgel too heavy for anyone else to lift, and amongst other talents he had the ability to change his form at will.

He had also wrung from the *Jade Emperor* the high sounding title *Great Sage Equal to Heaven* by which his temples today are still usually known. His *Buddhist* title, given him for his services to *Yuen Tsong*, is Buddha Victorious in Strife.

Spiritual Healing in the Temple in Sau Mau Ping

The festival takes place in the large playground of a low-cost housing estate near Kwun Tong in Kowloon. On the terrace at one end of the playground is a tiny temple inside which, tightly packed on a kind of reredos over the altar, are sculptures of all the protagonists in the story of the Journey to the West and a great many more *Buddhist* figures besides.

Here regularly on the 1st and 15th days of every moon Monkey manifests himself to believers by 'entering into' the body of a medium and 'speaking through' him.

On these occasions the medium, a man in his early forties, goes into trance and immediately takes on monkey-like characteristics — twitching, jumping,

Day 15
Mid-Autumn
Festival

Day 16
Monkey Festival

Day 16
Birthday of
Hau Wong
celebrated at
Tung Chung,
Lantau (see
Moon Six)

Day 27
Birthday of
Confucius

Also:
Day 23
Birthday of
Wong Tai Sin

Solar Calendar:
Autumn
Equinox
(usually 24th
September)

An exciting festival especially for the children — the Moon Festival. Lanterns are sold at paper shops which are all over Hong Kong. Many of them are made in China.

scratching, grinning. Together with his 'interpreter' (a man of some education) he then holds a clinic to which come people from many parts of Hong Kong with a large variety of illnesses. Each in turn explains his case to Monkey, who then diagnoses the disease, prescribes treatment, and gives advice through the mouth of his medium. Because the words the medium utters are not easily understandable, the 'interpreter' has always to be present to write down what is said.

The clientele is large, but the fees paid are very small: just a few cents handed over in a *red packet*. His followers say: 'The medium does not do it for money; that's how we know he is genuine.'

Fire Walking at the Festival

The festival in *Sau Mau Ping* is held on the day after the Moon Festival, a most propitious time for getting in touch with spirits. It could be described as an ordinary *god's* birthday party (see Moon Two and elsewhere) with special additions.

The 'additions' include an impressive display of supernatural powers, conveyed through the actions of three or four mediums in trance and an indeterminate number of devout believers.

Led by the chief medium dressed in yellow and red, the mediums demonstrate their invulnerability by sticking knives through their cheeks, cutting their tongues with razor sharp swords, washing in boiling oil, and climbing a tall ladder made of knives with the sharp edges turned upwards. Finally, followed by twenty or more believers — mostly young men, but in 1981 there was a girl among them — they run several times barefoot across a bed of red hot charcoal.

Afterwards, when their feet are examined, most are unmarked and the very few blisters that can be found are only small ones.

Blood from the sword cuts is splashed onto slips of green and yellow paper which are then used as talismans against sickness and evil of all kinds.

Day 27 Birthday of Confucius

Where to go: A ceremony is held on 27th September (Western calendar) at the Confucius Hall Middle School, Caroline Hill Road, Causeway Bay, Hong Kong. Write to the Master or telephone 5766 427 for further information.

Greatest Sage and Teacher

Confucius was born in 551 BC during the period of the Warring States. It was a time of great political turmoil and intense intellectual activity as learned men argued about different ideals of ethical and political philosophy, rather like Socrates and Plato in a somewhat similar political situation in Greece about a hundred years later.

Like Plato, too, Confucius developed the idea that good government could best be obtained if the governors themselves were trained in ethical philosophy, and in order to achieve such a goal he put his trust in education. Later centuries in China were to see Confucius' ideas put into practice. Alone among the traditional civilisations of the world, the Chinese placed the control of the government in the hands of meritocracy recruited by public examination, and the works of the great teacher became the basis of all traditional Chinese education. There can be no doubt that it is to these developments that China owes her uniquely long historical continuity. The system founded two centuries before the birth of Christ upon the Confucian basis lasted, not unaltered but fundamentally the same, right down to the twentieth century AD. It is no wonder that Confucius is revered as the greatest of all Chinese sages.

His system of ethics and politics was founded on the principle of 'virtue' which should characterize the behaviour of the 'good' and 'just' man. For some years he searched for an enlightened prince who would be willing to put his ideas into practice, but failing to find such a one he settled down to teaching and writing and ultimately through his books wielded a far greater influence.

Westerners will probably find *The Analects* the most accessible book to read. It is a collection of Confucius' sayings made by his students, in which his ideals of 'the mean', of 'balance' and 'harmony', and ethical principles that aim at the human heart as being the source of action are set out. It is impossible to summarize one of the greatest ethical systems in the world in a few lines, and readers who are interested are asked to turn to the list of suggested readings at the back .

The 'Monkey God' cuts his tongue with a sword during the festival. The potency of blood gives power to charms. Monkey God Festival, Sau Mau Ping.

A rare opportunity to see and be seen: Hakka countrywoman with a newly woven head-band at Lam Tsuen Ta Chiu celebration in 1981.

Taoist ceremony to counter the harmful symbolic effects of building a new highway. There are five rod-shaped charms ('fu'), one for each direction: East, South, West, North and Centre.

Moon Nine

Day 9 Ch'ung Yeung

Where to go: The same places are visited as at Ch'ing Ming (see Moon Three). For the custom of climbing hills, the top of the Peak is a favourite place, but all forms of public transport leading there are likely to be crowded. (Peak Tram, bus no. 15 from Central terminal, minibus from near the City Hall or taxi.) Alternatively, take the MTR to Tsuen Wan, then take bus no. 51 to Tai Mo Shan. Almost all the hills are popular for picnics today.

Autumn Remembrance

Ch'ung Yeung is the second annual family remembrance day, and much the same things are done as at the first, which is Ch'ing Ming (Moon Three). Whether a visit to the graves is made in the Spring or Autumn is a matter of family custom. In any case, both days are important times for family reunion. Special offerings are placed before the *ancestors* on the family shrines at home and there is a family dinner.

Clan Ceremonial

In the New Territories the male members of the biggest *clans* spend several days during the period of Ch'ing Ming or Ch'ung Yeung visiting the graves of all their founding *ancestors* in turn, cleaning gravestones, making offerings, and kneeling together to pay their respects. When all has been properly done, they sit down near the graves to share the sacramental food.

These are much bigger, more formal occasions than the family picnics described under Moon Three. Unlike the more immediate family dead, the *clan ancestors* lived long ago, and so their significance is no longer personal but symbolic. As the original forebears from whom all present are directly descended, they act as the focus of their loyalty to the past and to each other.

Clans do not exists in China anymore. Only in Taiwan and the New Territories of Hong Kong are these rituals still performed.

A Day for Climbing Hills

A story of the Han Dynasty (220 BC — 224 AD) tells how a virtuous scholar (*Woon King*) was warned one day of an impending disaster. Being a prudent man (like Noah in somewhat similar circumstances) he took care to heed the warning and hastened with his family to a high place in the nearby hills, taking food and a jug of chrysanthemum wine. When they returned home at the end of the day they found all their cattle and poultry lying dead and duly gave thanks for their escape.

It is possible that a much older custom lies behind this charming story, but if so, it is long forgotten. The people who picnic in the hills today and drink chrysanthemum wine do so in memory of the wise scholar.

The picnics include little cakes whose name (ko) is a pun on the word for top (ko) as a sign of hope that he who eats such a cake will gain promotion to the top. The same idea urges the young to scramble to the top of the hill before they turn for home.

In Hong Kong the day for Autumn Remembrance coincides with the day for Climbing Hills, but in central and northern China these two occasions were divided. There, hill climbing took place on the Double Ninth as in Hong Kong, and grave visiting was on the first day of Moon Ten.

Day 19 Remembrance of Koon Yam

Where to go: Certain *Buddhist* establishments celebrate all three dates. Public *gods'* birthday festivals are held at Kwu Tung on the 19th day of the Second Moon (train to Fanling, then taxi) and at Pak Sha Wan (Hebe Haven) on the 19th day of the Sixth Moon (MTR to Choi Hung, then bus no. 92, minibus or taxi).

Goddess of Mercy

Koon Yam, more usually known in English by the Mandarin pronunciation of her name Kwan Yin, is the *Buddhist* Goddess of Mercy. Innumerable legends exist about her, and she is so popular that her image is almost as often seen in *Taoist* temples as in *Buddhist* ones.

So popular, too, that all three of the possible days for commemorating her are remembered: her birthday on the 19th of the Second Moon, the day of her enlightenment on the 19th of the Sixth Moon and the day of her death on the 19th of the Ninth Moon.

Day 9
Ch'ung Yeung

Day 19
Remembrance
of Koon Yam

Also:
Day 28
Birthday of *Wah Kwong Shih Fu*

Clan offerings to the ancestors during the Ch'ung Yeung Festival, Ko Lau Wan in Sai Kung. Offerings include: roasted pig, bowls of cooked rice, vegetarian food, fruits and cups of tea and wine. Spirit money is also offered and then scattered in all directions.

At her wedding the bride must offer tea to all her new in-laws. In return they will give her red packets with 'lucky money' inside and presents to add to the gold jewellery she has already received.

酬謝神恩
太
林村鄉
太平清醮
酬謝神恩
敬賀
村鄉
太平清醮
酬謝神恩
敬賀
青田

Moon Ten & Eleven

A Closed Season for Festivals

The Chinese almanac was originally made to suit the cold winter of the North where the Tenth Moon saw the first falls of snow. That is why there are very few festivals in the Tenth, Eleventh and Twelfth Moons though the weather in Hong Kong remains serenely warm and sunny day after day. However, the gap is filled to some extent by weddings for which these months are very popular.

Until about thirty years ago village weddings in Hong Kong still followed the old customs. A bride was always carried from her parental home to that of her future father-in-law in a red sedan chair, even if sometimes the chair (with the bride inside) was taken most of the way by lorry.

Today she goes in a motor car. Wedding cars have red and yellow, not white ribbons, and a large girl doll is fixed to the radiator in front. And brides today wear white.

But white is the traditional mourning colour in China and no Hong Kong brides would risk wearing anything so unlucky all the time. So at the wedding feast in the evening, when bride and groom circulate among the many round tables to toast and be toasted by their guests, she wears traditional red.

Moon Eleven: Winter Solstice

Where to go: In the city this is almost exclusively a home event with little for the festival watcher to see. If you are visiting the countryside, look out for small groups of people making offerings to sacred trees and rocks.

The Imperial Ceremonies at the Temple of Heaven, Peking

The Winter Solstice is the true solar New Year.

In the northern hemisphere it is the shortest day. From now on, the hours of light begin to lengthen and everybody knows that in time spring must come again. All ancient civilizations marked this day with ritual of some kind.

Under the monarchy in China, it was the day on which the Emperor led the annual sacrifices at the Temple of Heaven in Peking. No foreigners, and very few Chinese were ever permitted to see this greatest of all Imperial ceremonies. Indeed, the ordinary people of the capital were obliged to stay at home and curtains were hung across the entrances to the lanes where they lived so that the Emperor's procession could pass along the main thoroughfares without danger of his being seen.

After the fall of the monarchy in 1912, the Imperial rites were abandoned, but in Hong Kong the people still treat the Winter Solstice as a day for staying at home, making offerings to the *ancestors*, and enjoying a family dinner.

In many villages in the New Territories there are ceremonial offerings in the temples or *ancestral halls*, followed by a distribution of pork. The small shrines to T'o Tei Kung are not forgotten (see Moon Two), and people also use this day for making offerings to spiritually powerful trees and rocks (see Moon One).

Day Varies: Ta Chiu, Taoist Festivals of Peace and Renewal

Where to go: These festivals take place in the New Territories at 3-, 5-, 7-, 10-, and even 30- or 60-year intervals. The major events of each festival occupy between three and five days in the Eleventh or Twelfth lunar month. The dates are not fixed but selected each time by divination. The location varies but Ta Chiu is celebrated somewhere every year.

The Rite of Cosmic Renewal

Literally the words Ta Chiu mean 'arrange sacrifices', but the *Taoist* festivals in the New Territories called Ta Chiu are much more than that. Their objective is no less than the wiping away of evil, the restoration of peace, and the renewal of life for the entire population of a sizeable group of villages.

A feature of the modern situation is the return of hundreds of emigrants from overseas 'Because we want our children to know our old customs...'

Together with the humans, two kinds of spirits are invited to the festival: *gods* and *ghosts*. The *ghosts* are the same suffering spirits for whom the Hungry Ghosts Festival of the Seventh Moon is held; the *gods* are of two different categories.

First in the minds of the villagers are the *gods* they know, in other words all the *deities* whose images are in the temples or who are represented in pictures or writing on red paper on the many local shrines. These are the local *'patron saints'* to whom the people make offerings and give birthday parties, and who they believe (or partly believe) can cure them, protect them, and help them divine the future. Almost all the *gods* described

Moon Ten

Day 5
Birthday of
Bodhidarma
(or Tat Moh in Cantonese.
Not celebrated widely in Hong Kong)

Moon Eleven

Day varies
Ta Chiu
(dates chosen by divination)

Day varies
On Lung
(dates chosen by divination)

Solar Calendar:
Winter Solstice
(usually 21st or 22nd December)

Dancing unicorn pays a visit to the Ta Chiu, Lam Tsuen. Huge flower boards are erected all over the matsheds during the celebrations.

elsewhere in this book belong to this category. Most of them are deified human beings.

In addition to these *'patron saints'*, the *Taoists* postulate the existence of three far greater spirits — the *Three Pure Ones*. Though they have names, the *Three Pure Ones* are more accurately thought of as abstractions, pure spirit. They dwell in the stars, at the true source of life, beyond the reach of change or decay.

The true aim of a Ta Chiu is to invite these greater spirits down so that their superabounding power may be brought to bear upon the villagers in order to renew their lives in every particular and reinstate them in the Way (*Tao*) of cosmic harmony.

These are esoteric matters. Ordinary villagers, who know little or nothing about them, are content to leave the complicated rituals to the *Taoist* priests they employ to perform them. For themselves, they know they must make offerings to their own patron *gods*, renounce evil, do good deeds, and feed the hungry *ghosts*.

The ceremonies of Ta Chiu thus go on at several different levels at once. First, there are the highly complex rites for the *Three Pure Ones* performed by the *Taoist* priests in the temple. Second, there is an almost continuous process of offering which the people perform before the patron *deities* whose images have been brought out of the temple and installed in a temporary *matshed* shrine for the occasion. This part of the ceremonies is very like a *god's* birthday festival, with operas too.

Third, there are a number of ceremonial occasions for communal good deeds. For example, there is a symbolic giving of life by liberating a large number of small caged birds, a similar liberation of fishes, and recurrent invitations to the hungry *ghosts*.

Fourth, there is purification. Cleansing of the altar was performed by the *Taoists* at the beginning of the festival. On a personal level, the evening before the festival opens, everyone has a bath and puts on clean clothes. From then until the end there should be no sexual intercourse and no meat eaten in any of the participating villages. Then on the very last morning there is a symbolic casting out of evil when the *Taoist* priests go from house to house collecting 'dirty' objects in a large paper boat which is later taken outside the bounds of the village and burned with all its contents.

Finally, on the last two nights, there are two spectacular closing ceremonies. First the Taoists read out to the *gods* the names of all member villagers, after which they send the huge list to heaven in flames on the back of a paper horse and then post a red paper duplicate list on a wall for all to see. Then, at midnight on the last night, the *Taoists* preside over an enormous 'clothes burning' at which the hungry *ghosts* are fed, clothed, given money, and sent away with the help of *Taai Si Wong*, similar to the ceremonies in the Seventh Moon.

Then, and only then, is the vegetarian fast broken and all the villagers together eat a joyous communal meal at which the meat of the *'golden pigs'*, offered previously to the *gods*, takes pride of place.

The scale of these ceremonies is often impressive. At Lam Tsuen in 1981 twenty-three villages took part, the *matshed* theatre had seats for more than three thousand people, more than a thousand travelled back from Europe, and the name list totalled nearly 7,000. As for the expenses, they topped HK$200,000.

Day Varies: On Lung, Pacifying the Dragon

There are a few villages in the New Territories at which a less well-known set of ceremonies with much the same general objectives takes place at similarly wide-spaced intervals of time. The people call it 'On Lung', which means 'Pacifying the Dragon'. It seems to be connected with the theories of Chinese *geomancy* and it is believed that in the olden days, this set of ceremonies is performed within one month of a village first being established.

The officiants, called *Fa Si* (magicians) or Redheads because they wear red turbans instead of the black caps of the orthodox *Taoist* priests, dance, posture, and sing, occasionally blowing mournful blasts on a cow's horn, in a manner not approved by the orthodox. An odd feature of these ceremonies is that one of the *Fa Si* dresses as a woman and dances with 'her' partner.

Many of the features of Ta Chiu are present, such as fasting, and releasing living creatures, and a great 'clothes burning' (see Moon Seven) with *Taai Si Wong* in charge. Then finally, on the fourth day, several small pots of food are buried on the hillside where the Dragon is said to reside overlooking the village and — now that he is pacified once more — hopefully protecting it.

These ceremonies are rare, and it seems that there are only two octogenarians who still know how to perform them. One of them lives in China.

Mr. Ch'e Kwai checks the list of names at the Ta Chiu, Lam Tsuen. The names of all who are regarded as member-villagers are written on this huge list which will be sent to heaven in flames on the back of a paper horse.

Quality Street

Top left and right — One of the Fa Si (magicians) puts on make-up and woman's clothes for the rituals. Bottom left — The male threatens the 'female' in the dance and 'she' crouches with 'her' fan. Bottom right — The high falsetto as 'she' performs 'her' rites in the form of dancing.

A village lady putting 'dirt' in the symbolic rubbish boat during the Lantern Festival in Sik Kong Wai, Yuen Long.

Children creep round and under Taai Si Wong's foot to gain health and courage.

Top two — Each dialect group has its own styles of paper sculpture. The blue-faced Taai Si Wong on the left is made by Ch'iu Chau people. Bottom right — A young boy creeps round and under Taai Si Wong's foot to gain health and courage. Bottom left — A tiger image pasted on the belly of the Taai Si Wong.

Following page: 'Taai Si Wong watching over the 'shiu yi' (burning clothes) ceremony at the end of the Hungry Ghosts Festival.

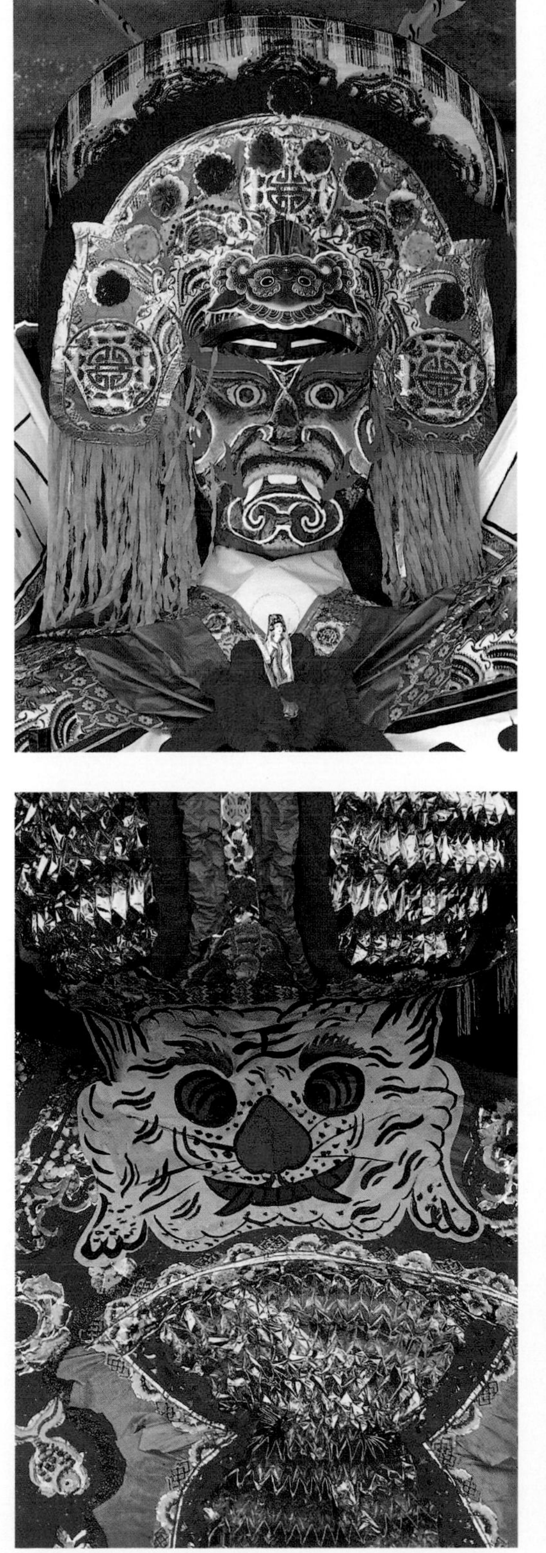

關帝宮

天后

Solar Calendar Chart

Nature has provided the earth with two obvious time markers — the sun and the moon. The huge majority of Chinese festivals are dated by the traditional lunar calendar as on the Chart of Festivals on the inside front and back covers. Lunar time being linked with the regular appearances of the full moon had certain obvious advantages for the organization of social life before the invention of modern artificial light. However, because the sun regulates the season, any agricultural civilization must use solar time to reckon its working year. The Gregorian calendar, used everywhere in the modern world, is a solar calendar, directly descended from the agricultural past of ancient Europe and the Middle East.

Ancient China had a solar calendar too. It was, and still is, used to regulate the agricultural year, and in the days of the imperial dynasties (before 1912) a large part of the Emperor's duty was to lead the rituals of the various great national festivals connected with it. The dates of two of these — Ch'ing Ming and the Winter Solstice — are regularly observed in contemporary Hong Kong.

Matching the Moon to the Sun

It seems to be quite easy for the same person to do his farming in terms of solar fortnights while regulating almost everything else by lunar months. Hong Kong's villagers do it all the time. But one reason why it is so easy is that the very difficult basic problems involved were dealt with by the ancient Chinese calendar makers at least three thousand years ago.

Hard though it was to solve, the puzzle they had to work out is easy to state:

> Given that one lunar month = 29.5 days (approximately)
> then 12 lunar months = 345 days (approximately)
> and given that one solar year = 365 days (approximately)

then the question is: what about the odd eleven days? Or, how can the two calendars be adjusted in such a way as to bring sun and moon reckoning into step?

In a greatly oversimplified way the solution that was found can be explained in terms of two theoretical discoveries and two practical steps, as follows:-

Discovery One: the eleven days left over between the end of a 345-day lunar year and a 365-day solar year can be partly 'mopped up' by adding in extra months now and then, thus making some lunar years 13 months long instead of 12. For example, if one extra moon month is added in three solar years the discrepancy between the solar calendar (3 x 365 = 1095 days) and the lunar calendar (12 + 12 + 13 moon months = 1091.5 days) is reduced to 3.5 days.

Step One: the practice of adding extra (intercalary) months like this was started very early indeed, probably before the year 1000 BC.

Discovery Two: before the eighth century BC it was also discovered that 19 complete years of solar time contained almost exactly the same number (6,840) of days as 235 complete months of lunar time. In other words, the movements of the sun and the moon which are naturally out of step if considered over the period of one year fall naturally into step over a period of 19 years.

With this knowledge it is easy to calculate that a remarkably good (though not quite exact) fit between the two calendars can be obtained by adding just seven extra moon months every 19 years.

Step Two: was simply the practical working out of the most useful way of doing this. Seven intercalary months were added in, most at three years, but some at two year intervals. For example, the lunar year more or less corresponding to 1982 has two Fourth Moons. Only the First, Eleventh and Twelfth Moons are never doubled.

It was also arranged that the Winter and Summer Solstices should always fall in the Eleventh and Fifth and the Spring and Autumn Equinoxes in the Second and Eighth Moons respectively.

Chart showing the twenty-four periods of the Chinese Solar Calendar: each period is approximately 15 days long

Name in English	Name in Chinese	Usual date in Gregorian calendar	Major imperial rites of the solar year in dynastic China
Beginning of spring	立春	February 5	Offerings in the Ta Miao (Great Temple)
Rain water	雨水	February 20	
Awakening from hibernation	驚蟄	March 6	
Spring equinox	春分	March 21	Offerings at the Temple of the Sun
Clear brightness	清明	April 5	Offerings at Imperial Tombs
Grain rain	穀雨	April 20	
Beginning of summer	立夏	May 6	Offerings in the Ta Miao
Small fullness (of grain)	小滿	May 21	
Grain in beard	芒種	June 6	
Summer solstice	夏至	June 22	Offerings at the Temple of the Earth
Small heat	小暑	July 7	
Great heat	大暑	July 23	
Beginning of autumn	立秋	August 8	Offerings in the Ta Miao
Limit of heat	處暑	August 23	
White dew	白露	September 8	
Autumn equinox	秋分	September 23	Offerings in the Temple of the Moon
Cold dew	寒露	October 8	
Frost descends	霜降	October 24	
Beginning of winter	立冬	November 8	Offerings in the Ta Miao
Small snow	小雪	November 22	
Great snow	大雪	December 7	
Winter solstice	冬至	December 22	Offerings in the Temple of Heaven
Small cold	小寒	January 6	
Great cold	大寒	January 21	

Glossary

The words and phrases italicized in the text are listed here in alphabetical order followed by the appropriate Chinese characters (and their Cantonese pronunciation in brackets, if not already given). Brief notes are added to explain the terms not covered in the text.

Ancestors: 祖先 (tso sin).

Ancestral Hall: 祠堂 (ch'i t'ong). Building maintained by members of one clan in memory of their joint ancestors.

Blocks, asking the: 問杯 (man pooi). See Moon One.

Boat People: 水上人 (sui seung yan). Water dwellers. Historically a despised group mainly in Kwangtung Province. Also known as Tanka (蜑家).

Boddhisatva: 菩薩 (p'o saat). Buddhist term for individual who has attained the highest levels of enlightenment but postponed his/her final absorption into Nirvana in order to help others along the way.

Bodhidarma: 達摩 First Buddhist patriarch of China, founder of the Ch'an (Zen) School of Buddhism.

Buddhism: 佛教 (faat kaau); Buddha: 佛祖 (faat tso).

Ch'an Kwan: 真君 Also known as Po Sheng 保生 literally 'protect life'. One of the gods of medicine.

Cheung T'in Si: 張天師 literally Heavenly Master Cheung. Title of Cheung To-ling 張道靈 a major figure in Taoism. Mandarin pronunciation Chang Tao-ling.

Ch'iu Chau: 潮洲 Dialect spoken in and around Swatow in northern Kwangtung Province. A person who speaks this dialect as his mother tongue. The second largest dialect group in Hong Kong (after Cantonese).

City God: 城隍 Every official walled city in Imperial China had a temple for the City God. Official ceremonies were held there.

Clan: 宗族 (dzung tsuk). Group of people descended in the male line from one common male ancestor and sharing an interest in common property (e.g. ancestral hall, land).

Dancing Lions: 舞獅 (mo si). Kind of masked dancing performed on propitious occasions. The words 'mo si' sound the same as a term meaning 'no trouble'.

Deities: 神 (shan). See Patron Saints.

Dragon Mother: 龍母 (lung mo). Popular for her ability to prevent disasters at sea and look after children. Mostly worshipped by women, especially Boat People.

Dzung Tsan Wooi: 宗親會 Clan association. See Clan.

Fa p'aau: 花炮 literally 'flowery rocket'. See Moon Two.

Fa si: 法師 Magician. Term used for unorthodox ('redhead') Taoist practitioners.

Flower board: 花牌 (fa p'ai). Decorated announcements erected over theatres, shops, restaurants etc. giving details about special occasions.

Flower festival: 花節 (fa tsit). An old practice of celebrating the day on which all flowers were believed to bloom. The flowers' 'birthday'. Observed more in North China than in the South.

Foods, special: Like most other people, the Chinese link their festivals with the eating of certain special foods. Here are some examples from Hong Kong. At **New Year:** year cakes (nin ko 年糕 . The word 'ko' means 'high' or 'progressive', 'nin' means 'year'; thus 'nin ko' implies progress and prosperity for the year); round sesame seed cakes (tsin tui 煎堆 . There is a Cantonese rhyme which can be translated 'As the sesame cakes are rolled, the house is filled with silver and gold'); Dried oyster (ho si 蠔豉 . These words sound like 'good sales' so businessmen and shopkeepers naturally like them); Fish (yue 魚 , which sounds like another word written with another character meaning 'profit' or 'surplus'); Sweet snacks of various kinds, indicating a sense of sweetness. At the **Lantern Festival:** small, round, sweet dumplings (tong yuen, 湯丸 implying 'rounded sweetness', or a sweet, harmonious life together). At **Ch'ing Ming:** bean curd with fish heads and tails. Fish indicates 'profit', heads and tails imply a sense of wholeness; the word 'fu' in 'tao fu' 豆腐 (bean curd) also sounds rather like the word 'wu' (護) which means 'protect'. The hope is that the ancestors will protect their descendants. **Dragon Boat Festival:** rice-dumplings (chung tsi 糉子) (see Moon Five). **Hungry Ghosts Festival:** no special foods are eaten. Instead of a chicken, a duck is more commonly used in offerings since it is feared that the sharp beak and claws of a chicken might damage the clothes that are to be sent to the ghosts. **Mid-Autumn Festival:** moon cakes (yuet beng 月餅). Their round shape denotes a sense of completeness and togetherness, and mirrors the roundness of the full moon.

Fortune Sticks, shaking the: 求簽 (k'ao ch'im). See reading list, book on Man Mo Temple.

Fu: 符 Charm, talisman.

Geomancy, Chinese: 風水 (fung shui: literally, wind and water). Theory of the forces underlying such natural phenomena as hills, watercourses, certain directions, etc. which affect human fate and therefore must be taken into careful consideration in choosing sites for graves, temples and all buildings.

Ghosts: 鬼 (kwai). Disembodied spirits.

Ginger: 薑 (keung). A strongly 'yang' foodstuff traditionally eaten by women after childbirth. Hence a propitious symbol.

God, Goddess: 神 (shan). See Patron Saints.

Golden Pagodas: 金塔 (kam taap). Euphemistic term for ceramic pot about two feet high in which bones of ancestors are carefully placed after exhumation. Exhumation normally takes place seven years after the first burial and may be followed by reburial in a final tomb later. The practice of secondary burial is a southern Chinese custom, not found elsewhere in China.

Golden Pigs: 金豬 (kam chue). Whole roast pigs offered to gods and spirits. The meat is eaten later and considered not only especially delicious but also potently efficacious against sickness and all manner of ill-fortune.

Great Sage Equal to Heaven: 齊天大聖 (ch'ai t'in tai shing). Literally 'Holy Saint Equal to Heaven'.

Hakka: 客家 literally, 'guest families'. Dialect of Chinese spoken in northern and eastern Kwangtung Province and also in Taiwan and elsewhere. A person who speaks this dialect as his mother tongue. The majority of the population in the eastern New Territories are Hakka.

Hoklo: 鶴佬 Immigrants and descendants of immigrants from the southern part of Fukien Province. Closely related to early Chinese immigrants into Taiwan (Taiwanese). Dialect spoken by these people as their mother tongue.

Immortals, Eight: 八仙 (paat shin). Sometimes misleadingly translated 'Eight Fairies'. A true Taoist adept does not die but becomes transformed into an Immortal (e.g. Lu Pan, Moon Six). The number of Taoist immortals is very large, but there is a group of Eight who are especially famous and much loved. See reading list.

Jade Emperor: 玉皇 (yuk wong). Head of the Taoist pantheon of 'saints'. See Patron Saints and Three Pure Ones.

K'ai Fong Wooi: 街坊會 Neighbourhood club.

K'am Fa: 金花 Goddess responsible for giving safe delivery and care of babies.

Kung Fu: 功夫 Well-known Chinese term for 'boxing'; or any other ability acquired through discipline.

Kwangtung Province (Guangdong): 廣東省 Southeastern seaboard province of China. Hong Kong, Kowloon and the New Territories are geographically and culturally a part of Kwangtung Province. Kwangtung is more commonly rendered as Canton, and the dialect is usually called Cantonese.

Kwoh Nin: 過年 literally, 'crossing the year'. A common term for New Year. An ancient story tells of a fearsome monster called Nin who prowled the earth on the last night of every year. He was finally frightened away with loud noises and bright colours, which explains why people let off firecrackers and put up red papers on New Year's Eve.

Lettuce: 生菜 (shang ts'oi). The words mean literally 'life vegetable' which is a propitious meaning in itself, but as ts'oi sounds just like a word that means 'riches' the implication is doubly fortunate. Dancing Lions are given whole lettuce plants to 'eat' and the plants are also hung on the fa p'aau and elsewhere as charms.

Lu Ting-pin: 呂洞賓 One of the Eight Immortals.

Lucky Money: 利是 (lai si). See Moon One.

Man Ch'eung: 文昌 God in charge of examinations and fate. Traditionally worshipped by scholars and students.

Matshed: 棚 (p'aang). Temporary building made of bamboo poles and roofed with matting. Very large ones are erected as theatres for opera performances (matshed theatres); smaller ones are used as 'temporary temples' or 'shrines' at public festivals. Modern fire regulations have led to zinc sheets being used instead of matting.

Mei Ah: 尾禡 The final '16th day' (see Moon Two) ceremonies of the year and the day on which the household gods are sent back to Heaven (see Moon Twelve, for Kitchen God who is the last to go). Celebrated by some families and groups with an annual dinner and thanksgiving to gods.

Mencius: 孟子 (maan tsi). Scholar and philosopher ranked second only to Confucius. His day is celebrated in Hong Kong by the Confucius Association in conjunction with Mother's Day. (Mencius' mother won eternal fame in China for the way in which she brought up her son.)

Opening the Light: 開光 (hoi kwong). The image of a god or sacred creature of any kind is considered incomplete (not 'alive') until this ceremony has been performed. Page 57 show image of T'o Tei Kung with eyes bandaged awaiting 'hoi kwong'. See Moon Five.

Patron Saints: The gods of popular Taoism. Most of them are deified human beings and nearly all are patron deities of particular places, persons, or trades. These gods are grouped into an elaborate bureaucratic hierarchy under the Jade Emperor. Known in Taoism as Gods of the 'Posterior Heavens' (and far inferior to the Three Pure Ones) they are subject to change and therefore to the alternations of yin and yang.

Phoenix: 鳳凰 (fun wong). The Phoenix is normally taken to be the complement of the Dragon, yin rather than yang, and therefore appropriate for females. The Emperor was the 'Dragon', the Empress the 'Phoenix'. Both dragon and phoenix are mythical creatures with powerful symbolic meaning.

Po Sheng Ta Tai: 保生大帝 Literally 'Protect Life Emperor'. See Ch'an Kwan.

Primordial Deity: See Three Pure Ones.

Queen Mother of the Western Heaven: 西天皇母 (Sai T'in Wong Mo). Leading figure in the Taoist pantheon of saints. See Patron Saints.

Red Packets: 紅包 (hung pao). See Moon One.

Sau Mau Ping: Address for Monkey Festival in Moon Eight: Sau Ming Road Playground.
九龍秀茂坪秀明道球場

Sham Shan Kwok Wong: 三山國王 The gods of three famous mountains in the Ch'iu Chau region of northern Kwangtung. Said to have helped to pacify this area in the T'ang Dynasty (618–907 AD).

Shiu Yi: 燒衣 literally 'burning clothes'.

Sonaat: 嗩吶 Woodwind instrument, oboe type, with reed.

Spirit Money: 元寶 (yuen po). 'Pretend' paper money used in offerings to gods and spirits and sent to them by burning. There are various kinds: squares of plain brownish paper; rectangles printed with 'gold' and 'silver' lines and often made up into 'ingots'; notes printed on 'The Bank of Hell' (usually misspelled 'Held') in large denominations. All available at religious paper shops.

Star Gods: 星君 (shing kwan). The Taoists have translated many of their patron saints (q.v.) to the skies. Some of the Star Gods are so important that they are honoured with separate birthdays, but all are included in the general remembrance in Moon One.

Taai Si Wong: 大士王 See Moon Seven.

Tao, Taoist: 道 Tao (Cantonese pronunciation: to) literally means 'the way'. Taoism is the ancient religion indigenous to China which co-existed over the centuries with Confucianism and Mahayana Buddhism (the so-called 'three religions of China'). Over the several thousand years since its beginning, Taoism developed many sides which included, at one extreme, a sophisticated philosophical system and a highly metaphysical type of disciplined mysticism and, at the other, the strongly materialistic rituals of popular Taoism with its multitude of 'patron saints' deities, some of whose 'birthday' celebrations are described in this book. Taoist theories are the basis of traditional Chinese cosmology. See also Moon Eleven, Yin and Yang, and reading list.

Tei Chong Wong: 地藏王 One of the gods of Hell. Helps to get rid of evil and avert disasters.

Three Pure Ones: 三清 (sham ch'ing). The three highest Taoist divinities: Primordial Heavenly Worthy, Lord of Heaven; Ling-Po Heavenly Worthy, Lord of Earth; To-tak Heavenly Worthy, Lord of Man. These three are gods of the 'Prior Heavens', beyond the reach of change. See also Moon Eleven and reading list.

Ts'oi Pak Shing Kwan: 財帛星君 One of the Gods of Wealth.

T'ung Heung Wooi: 同鄉會 An association with members from the same place of origin or village.

T'ung T'in Ling Mo: 通天靈帽 Literally 'Potent Hat for reaching Heaven'.

Unicorns: 麒麟 (k'ei lun). The Unicorn is another of the mythical propitious beasts. Unicorn masks are used (mainly by Hakka village kung fu clubs) for masked dancing, like the Dancing Lions.

Wah Kwong Shih Fu: 華光師傅 Patron deity of Cantonese opera troupes.

Wah T'o: 華陀 A famous doctor of the era of the Romance of the Three Kingdoms. Excelled at acupuncture and surgery. Worshipped by traditional Chinese doctors and herbalists.

Wat Yuen: 屈原 Mandarin pronunciation: Chu Yuan. See Moon Five.

Wong Tai Sin: 黃大仙 Local deity with one of the largest and most popular temples in Kowloon. Renowned for the accuracy of his predictions, and said to be able to make every wish come true. His busy and elaborate temple in Kowloon (MTR Wong Tai Sin station) should most certainly be visited.

Woon King: 桓景 Mandarin pronunciation: Huan Jing. See Moon Nine.

Yamen: 衙門 (This is the Mandarin pronunciation. Cantonese is 'ngamoon'.) Magistrate's court; official residence; official building, etc. in Imperial China.

Yan Yat: 人日 The seventh day of the New Year. Human Being's Day, when everyone adds an extra year of age to his total. Each of the first ten days of the year is an 'anniversary' for one or other of the domestic animals or products. The first is chickens' day, the second dogs' day, then pigs', ducks', oxen, horses', humans', rice, fruit-and-vegetables', and wheat-and-barley, in that order.

Yi Wu: 二胡 (Mandarin: Erh Hu). Chinese two-string violin.

Yim Lo Wong: 閻羅王 Buddhist King of Hell. Mandarin pronunciation: Yen Lo Wong.

Yin and Yang: 陰陽 (Cantonese pronunciation: Yam and Yeung). Traditionally Chinese cosmological thinking posits the existence of two complementary forces, the constant alternation of which produces all life, movement, and change in the universe. Yin is variously described as cool, dark, damp, feminine, the moon, etc. and Yang as hot, bright, dry, masculine, the sun, etc. Their alternation is exemplified in the annual cycle beginning on the day of the Winter Solstice when Yang begins to increase, onwards to its peak on the day of the Summer Solstice. Immediately on that day, Yin in turn begins to grow at Yang's expense, until on reaching the Winter Solstice again Yin is at its height and at that very moment Yang starts to increase once more. Similarly in every month the days from the first to the fifteenth (when the Moon is full) see an ever-increasing Yin, and then immediately and automatically, from the fifteenth onwards to the end of the Moon, Yang in turn takes over. Virtually the whole of traditional Chinese cosmological thought, including alchemy, medicine and art, hangs on the theory of Yin and Yang, their constant alternation, and achievement of balance between them.

Yuen Tsong: 玄奘 Mandarin pronunciation: Hsuan Tsang. See Moon Eight.

Zodiac, Chinese: See reading list.

Suggested Additional Reading

Author	Title	Publisher	Year
Hugh D.R. Baker	Ancestral Images	South China Morning Post, Hong Kong	1979
	More Ancestral Images	South China Morning Post, Hong Kong	1980
	Ancestral Images Again	South China Morning Post, Hong Kong	1981
V.R. Burkhardt	Chinese Creeds and Customs (originally published in 3 volumes 1955–1959)	South China Morning Post, Hong Kong	1982
Juliet Bredon and Igor Mitrophanow	The Moon Year (originally published in 1927)	Paragon Books Reprint Corporation, New York	1966
S.T. Cheung	Fortune Stick Predictions, Man Mo Temple	The Tung Wah Group of Hospitals, Hong Kong	1982
Anthony Christie	Chinese Mythology	Hamlyn, London	1966
Confucius (translated by D.C. Lau)	The Analects	Penguin Books, London	1979
Wolfram Eberhard	Chinese Festivals	Schumm, New York (also The Oriental Cultural Services, Taipei)	1952
David Faure	The Structure of Chinese Rural Society	Oxford University Press	1986
T.C. Lai	Animals of the Chinese Zodiac	Hong Kong Book Centre, Hong Kong	1982
	The Eight Immortals (originally published in 1972)	Swindon Book Company, Hong Kong	1977
Lo Kuan-chung (translated by Moss Roberts)	Three Kingdoms: China's Epic Drama	Pantheon Books, New York	1976
Michael R. Saso	Taoism and the Rite of Cosmic Renewal	Washington State University Press, Pullman	1972
Kristofer Schipper	Le Corps Taoiste	Paris	1982
Wu Ch'eng-en (translated by Arthur Waley)	Monkey (originally published in 1961)	Penguin Books, London	1977

Index

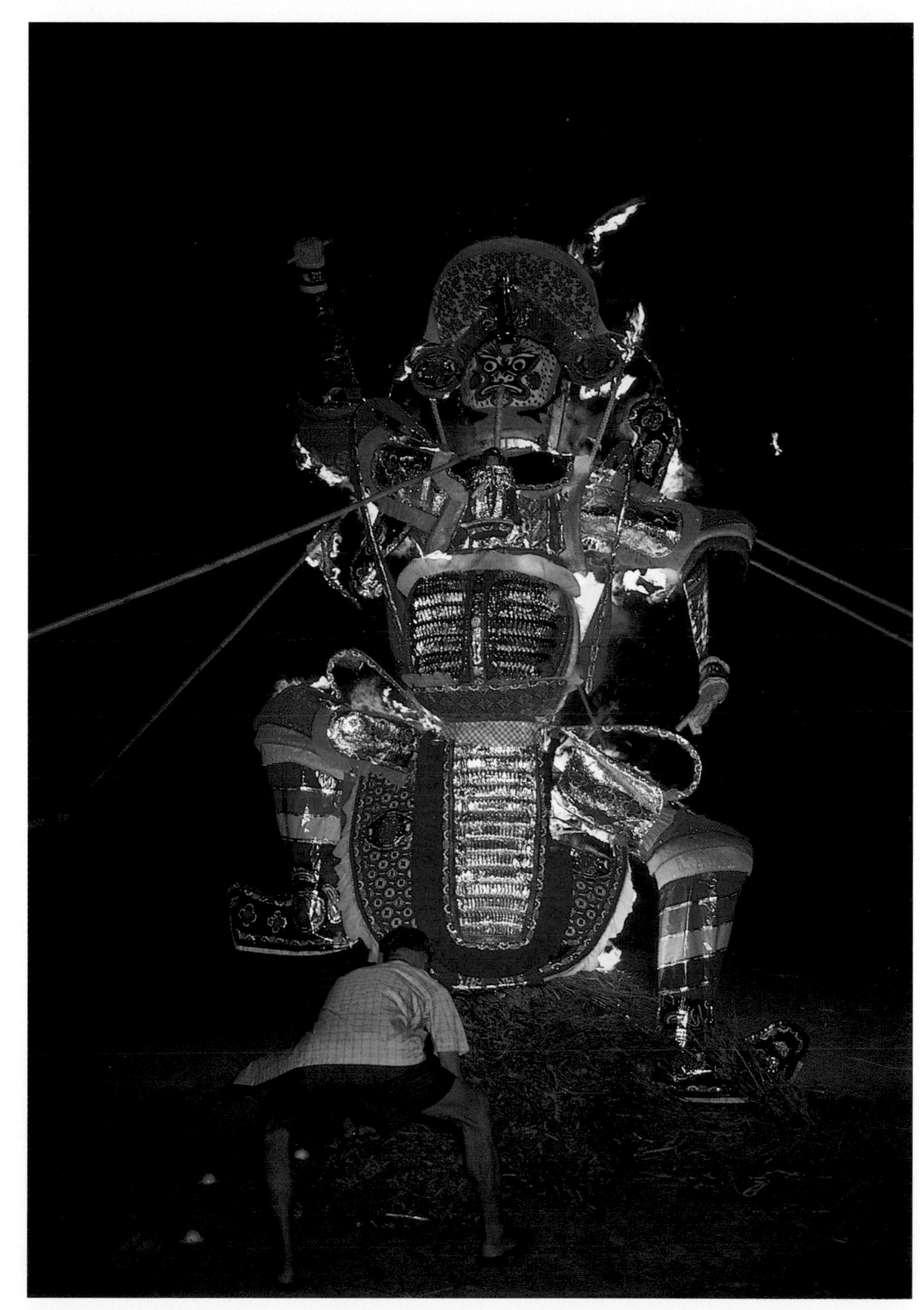

Taai Si Wong prepares to leave for Heaven in flames. He will take with him the local ghosts and the area will be cleared of potential trouble-makers.

Festival

Corresponding Dates in Solar Calendar						Lunar Dates		Name in English
1992	1993	1994	1995	1996	1997	Moon	Day	
Monkey	Cock	Dog	Pig	Rat	Ox			
28/1	16/1	4/2	24/1	12/2	1/2	12	24	Kitchen God Visits Heaven
4/2	23/1	10/2	31/1	19/2	7/2	1	1	New Year Festival
6/2	25/1	12/2	2/2	21/2	9/2		3	Birthday of Ch'e Kung
19/2	6/2	24/2	14/2	4/3	21/2		15	Lantern Festival
5/3	22/2	13/3	2/3	20/3	10/3	2	2	Birthday of T'o Tei Kung
16/3	5/3	24/3	13/3	31/3	21/3		13	Birthday of Hung Shing Kung
22/3	11/3 leap	30/3	19/3	6/4	27/3		19	Birthday of Koon Yam
4/4	5/4 3rd Moon	5/4	5/4	4/4	5/4	3		Ch'ing Ming Festival
5/4	25/3 (24/4)	13/4	2/4	20/4	9/4		3	Birthday of Pak Tai
25/4	14/4 (14/5)	3/5	22/4	10/5	29/4		23	Birthday of T'in Hau
Dates chosen by Divination						4		Cheung Chau Bun Festival
10/5	28/5	18/5	7/5	24/5	14/5		8	Birthday of Lord Buddha
10/5	28/5	18/5	7/5	24/5	14/5		8	Birthday of T'am Kung
5/6	24/6	13/6	2/6	20/6	9/6	5	5	Dragon Boat Festival
13/6	2/7	21/6	10/6	28/6	17/6		13	Birthday of Kwan Tai
5/7	24/7	14/7	3/7	21/7	10/7	6	6	Birthday of Hau Wong
12/7	31/7	21/7	10/7	28/7	17/7		13	Birthday of Lu Pan
18/7	6/8	27/7	16/7	3/8	23/7		19	Enlightenment of Koon Yam
5/8	24/8	13/8	2/8 leap	20/8	9/8	7	7	Seven Sisters' Festival
13/8	1/9	21/8	10/8 8th Moon	28/8	17/8		15	Hungry Ghosts Festival
11/9	30/9	20/9	9/9 (9/10)	27/9	16/9	8	15	Mid-Autumn Festival
12/9	1/10	21/9	10/9 (10/10)	28/9	17/9		16	Monkey God Festival
23/9	12/10	2/10	21/9 (21/10)	9/10	28/9		27	Birthday of Confucius
4/10	23/10	13/10	1/11	20/10	10/10	9	9	Ch'ung Yeung Festival
14/10	2/12	23/10	11/11	30/10	20/10		19	Remembrance of Koon Yam
21/12	22/12	22/12	23/12	21/12	22/12	11		Winter Solstice
Dates chosen by Divination								Ta Chiu

GB	*God's birthday*
HG	*Hungry ghosts*
F	*Family*
A	*Ancestors*
B	*Birthday*

Calendar

Chinese Characters	Code		Corresponding Dates in Solar Calendar 1998 Tiger	1999 Rabbit	2000 Dragon	2001 Snake	2002 Horse	2003 Sheep	2004 Monkey
灶君節	F	h	22/1	9/2	30/1	18/1	5/2	26/1	15/1
農曆新年	F	h	28/1	16/2	5/2	24/1	12/2	1/2	22/1
車公誕	GB	p	30/1	18/2	7/2	26/1	14/2	3/2	24/1 leap
元宵			11/2	2/3	19/2	7/2	26/2	15/2	5/2 2nd Moon
土地誕	O	ph	28/2	19/3	7/3	24/2	15/3	4/3	21/2 (22/3)
洪聖誕	GB	p	11/3	30/3	18/3	7/3	26/3	15/3	3/3 (2/4)
觀音誕	GB	p	17/3	5/4	24/3	13/3	1/4	21/3	9/3 (8/4)
清明節	FA	o	5/4	5/4	4/4	5/4	5/4	5/4	4/4
北帝誕	GB	p	30/3	18/4	7/4	27/3 leap	15/4	4/4	21/4
大后誕	GB	p	19/4	8/5	27/4	16/4 4th Moon	5/5	24/4	11/5
長洲飽山節	HG	p	Dates chosen by Divination						
浴佛節	B	i	3/5 leap	22/5	11/5	30/4 (30/5)	19/5	8/5	26/5
譚公誕	GB	p	3/5 5th Moon	22/5	11/5	30/4 (30/5)	19/5	8/5	26/5
端午節	O	p	30/5 (28/6)	18/6	6/6	25/6	15/6	4/6	22/6
關帝誕	GB	p	7/6 (6/7)	26/6	14/6	3/7	23/6	12/6	30/6
侯王誕	GB	p	28/7	18/7	7/7	26/7	15/7	5/7	22/7
魯班誕	GB	i	4/8	25/7	14/7	2/8	22/7	12/7	29/7
觀音誕	GB	p	10/8	31/7	20/7	8/8	28/7	18/7	4/8
七姐節	O	h	28/8	17/8	6/8	25/8	15/8	4/8	22/8
盂蘭節	HG	p	5/9	25/8	14/8	2/9	23/8	12/8	30/8
中秋節	F	h	5/10	24/9	12/9	1/10	21/9	11/9	28/9
齊天大聖誕	O		6/10	25/9	13/9	2/10	22/9	12/9	29/9
孔聖誕	O	i	17/10	6/10	24/9	13/10	3/10	23/9	10/10
重陽節	FA		28/10	17/10	6/10	25/10	14/10	4/10	22/10
觀音誕	GB	p	7/11	27/10	16/10	4/11	24/10	14/10	1/11
冬至	F	h	22/12	22/12	21/12	22/12	22/12	22/12	21/12
太平清醮	HG	p	Dates chosen by Divination						

o *Others*
p *Public*
h *Home*
i *Institution*